Table of Conte

Introduction

The Stories

Stories are provided at a variety of levels ranging from simple, predictable text for emerging readers to more complex text. All of the stories include a Story Dictionary and illustrations to support the text.

Reproduce the stories and prepare story booklets for individual students. There are many possible ways to share the stories:

- read the stories together
- have small groups of students read the stories
- have partners read a story together, or
- have individuals read the stories independently

Skill Pages

Use the skill pages following the stories

- to assess students' comprehension
- to teach and practice decoding skills
- to reinforce phonics instruction, and
- to provide opportunities for students to write new words and to use new sentence structures

Previewing a Story (Prereading)

Before giving a new independent reading story to a student or a group of students, take time to develop a context of experiences that will help your readers to succeed.

1. Read the title and help your students to connect it to their experiences. For example:
   "The title of this story is *At the Amusement Park.* Have you ever been to an amusement park? What did you see there? What did you do?"

2. Preview the story with the readers.
   - Look first at the words presented in the Story Dictionary.
     "Who can use the Story Dictionary to read the new words from the story?"
   - Then page through the story together. Have the readers look at the illustrations and predict what they think is happening on the pages. Listen closely to the vocabulary used. Suggest words and phrases that are used in the story vocabulary that might be unfamiliar to the readers. (See page 3 for a list of words and phrases for each story in this book.)
     "If you went to an amusement park, what would you see?"
     "Yes, you would see rides like roller coasters, ticket windows, crowds, and loudspeakers."
   - You may want to write the words as you talk about them, or ask the readers to locate the words on a specific page.
     "Can you find the words 'dark tunnels' on this page?"

Words to Talk About

As you preview the stories for beginning readers, be sure to point out the following words and phrases not found in the story dictionaries.

Story	Words
A Pair Is Two	pair, clothes
Breakfast in Bed	here, fill, take it away, breakfast, Sleepyhead
Put It In	put, nickel
Josh's Bike	red, fast, wobbles, zips past
The Egg Search	where, best, Annie, Peanut, Butter, three, hens
Just Sleeping	sleeping, waiting, open, dreams, friends, there, little, floor, bed, fill, head
Strike Up the Band	blow, bang, join, won't, grand
My Puppy Snickers	explore, meets, nibble, snuggles, nap, loves
Isn't It?	can't, oh, gosh, ooo, isn't
Mr. Scarecrow	stuffed, fat, stood, welcome, friends, everywhere
What Do I See?	little, playing, Daddy's knee
The Same and Not the Same	planted, same, great-grandpa, grandpa, dad, picked, ate, snack
The Hole That Matt Dug	dug, rolled, heard, bark, found
Mr. Snowman	shape, roll, another, more, just, twig
I Can See the Moon	flash, honk, rumbles by, nighttime, whinny softly, perch, coop, loud, quiet, busy, still
At the Amusement Park	zipped, yelled, answered, chugged, dark, boomed, closing, race, leave, wait, don't
Traveling	going, biking, street, riding, sleeping, flying, traveling
The Candy Store	buy, chocolate, sugar, stomach is growling, taste, smell, ready, sweet, surprise
Things to Do	plant, fly, kick, out of sight, walk, ride, pick up, hike, outside, adventure, agree
Simple Machines	simple machines, work, lift, heavy, cut apart, hold together, moving, easy, ramp, every day
Recycling	used, usable, energy
The Hippopotamus	rivers, lakes, Africa, spends, water, resting, underwater, bottom, minutes

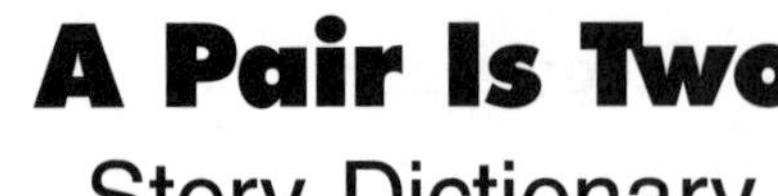

A Pair Is Two

Story Dictionary

1

socks

shoes

mittens

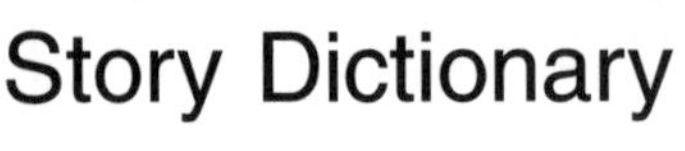

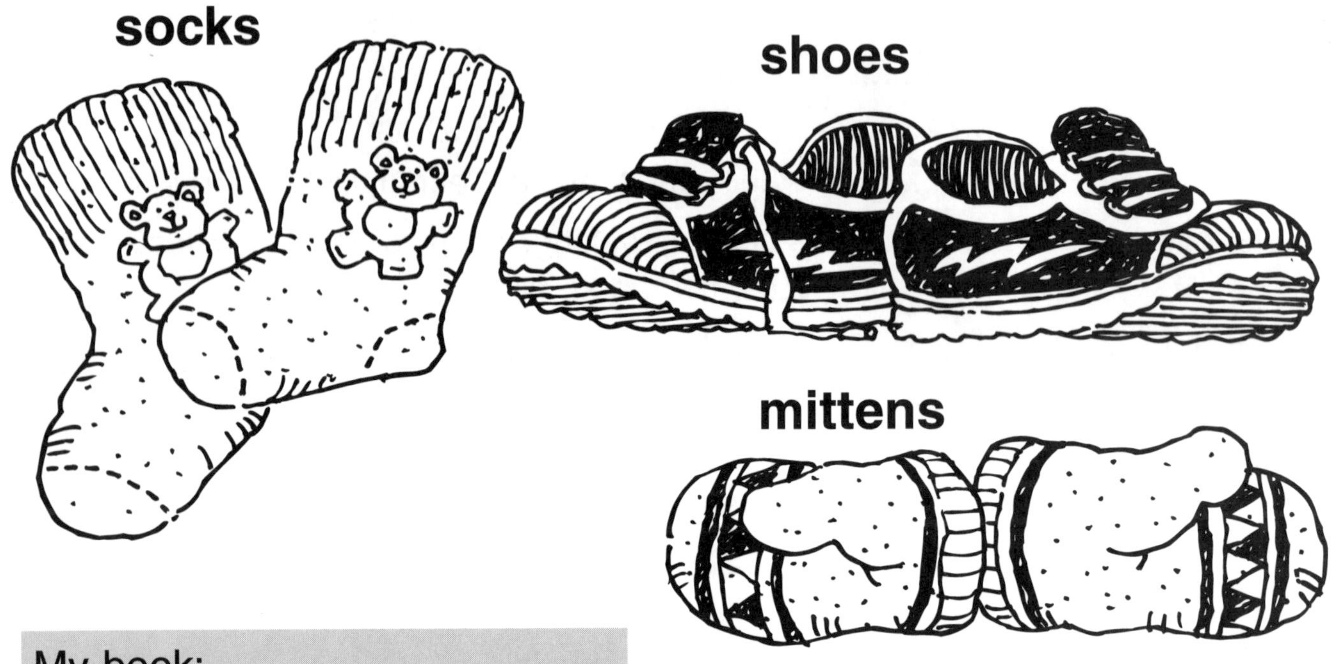

My book:

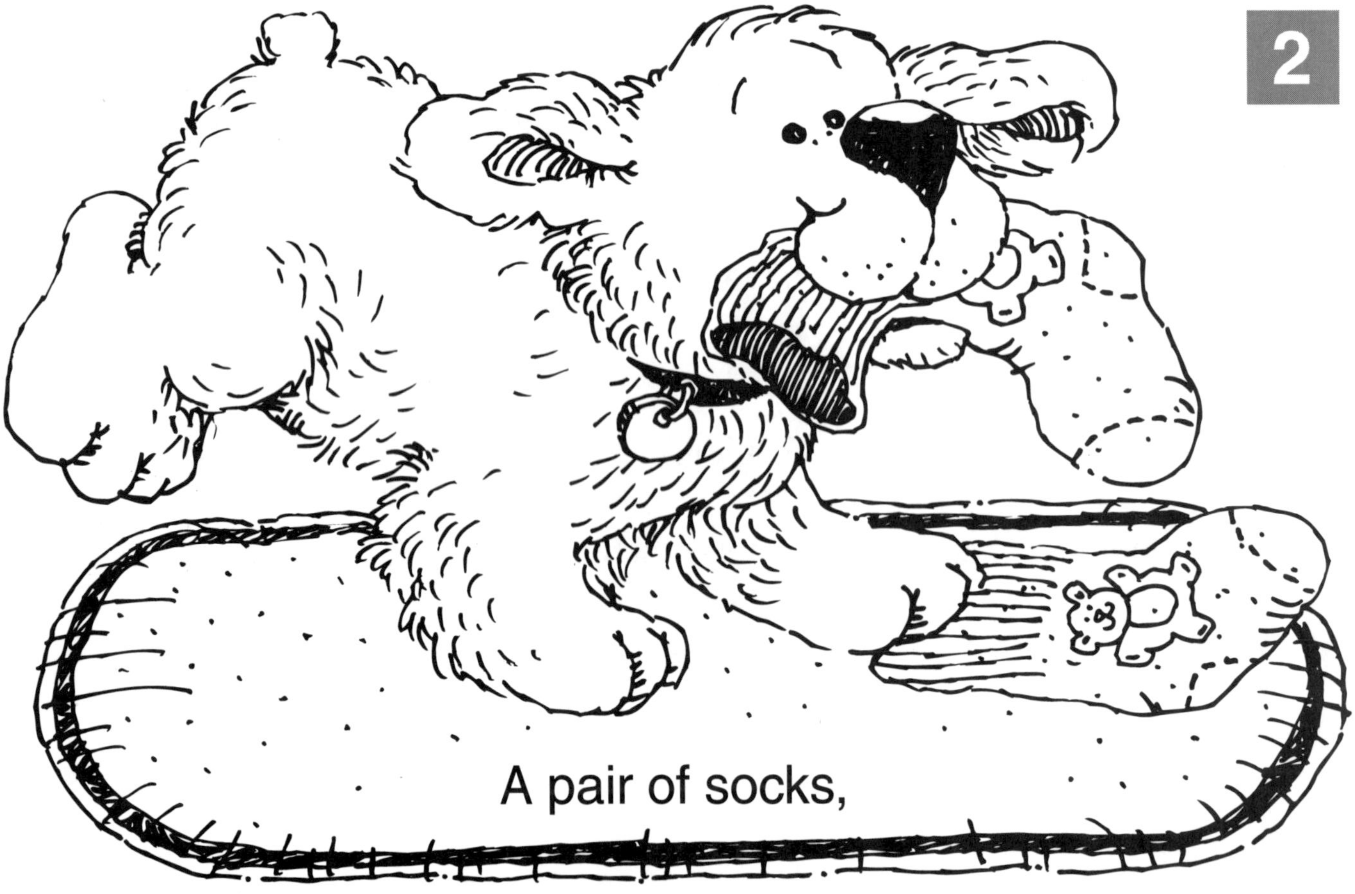

2

A pair of socks,

3

A pair of shoes,

4

A pair of mittens:
My clothes—in twos!

EMC 745 5

©1999 by Evan-Moor Corp.

Name ______________________________

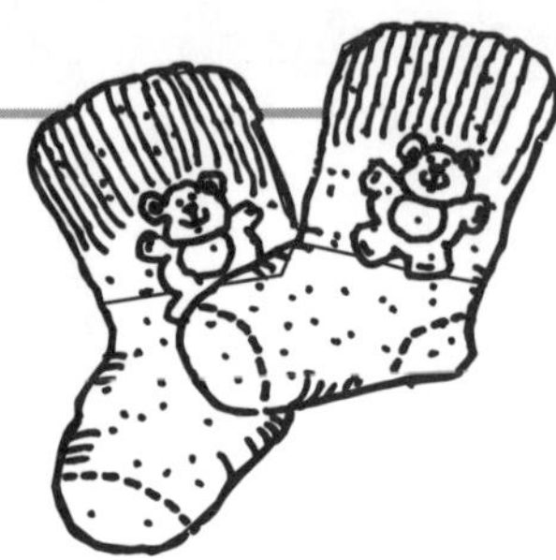

What Did the Story Say?

Draw the three pairs of things that belonged to the boy in the story.

1.	2.
3.	Draw a pair of things that belong to you.

Name ____________________

Working with Word Families

-ock

Write the word. Draw to show what each word means.

r + ock =	d + ock =
___ ___ ___ ___	___ ___ ___ ___
l + ock =	bl + ock =
___ ___ ___ ___	___ ___ ___ ___ ___
s + ock =	cl + ock =
___ ___ ___ ___	___ ___ ___ ___ ___

Name ______________________________

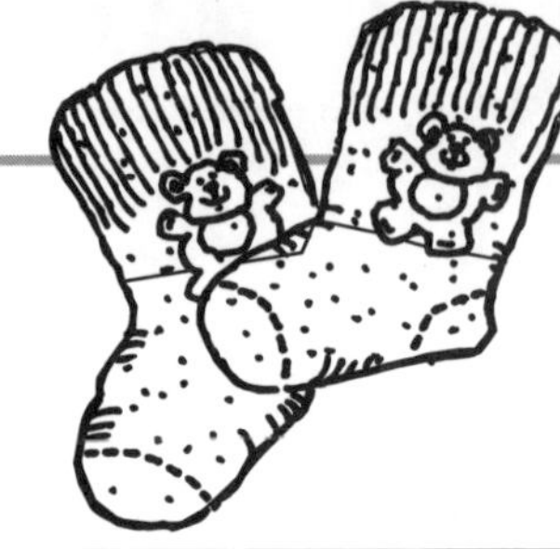

Rhyming Pairs

Color, cut, and paste to show pairs that rhyme.

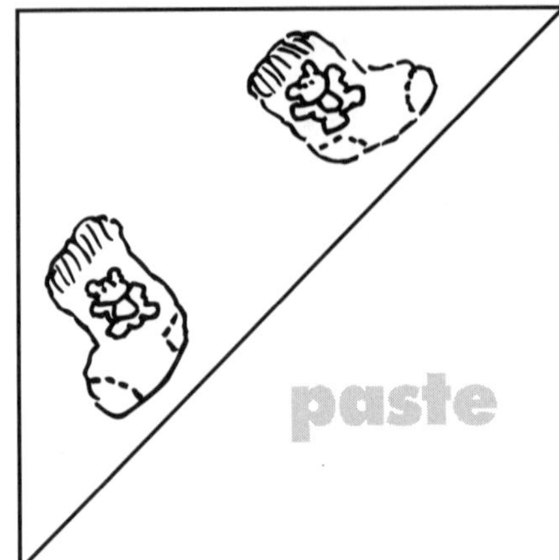

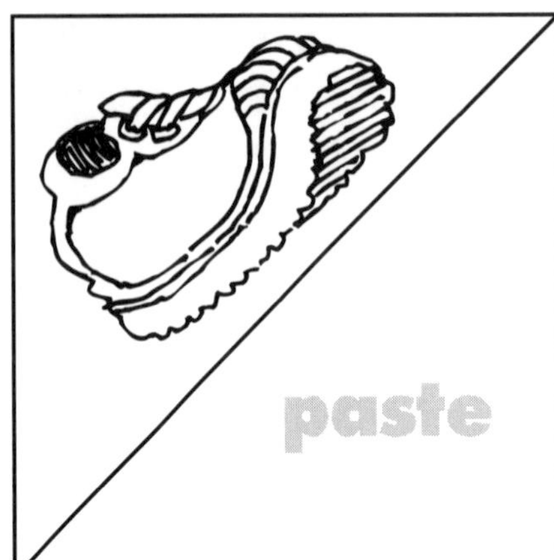

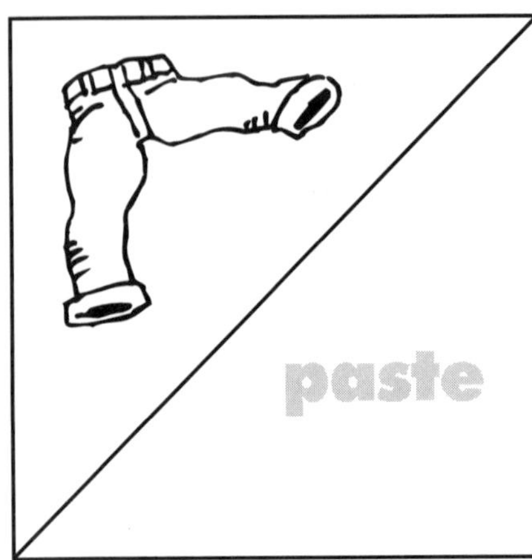

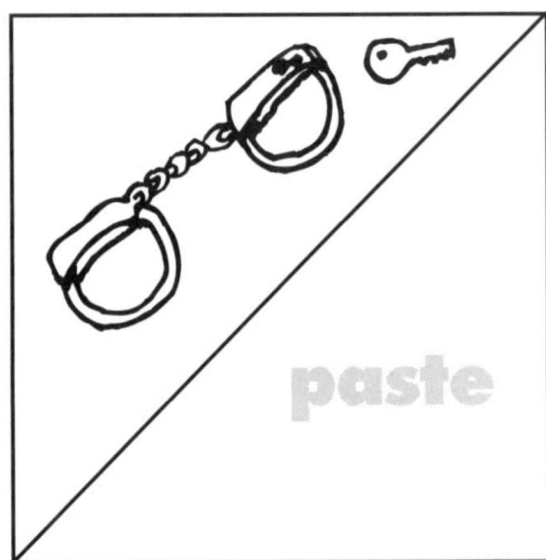

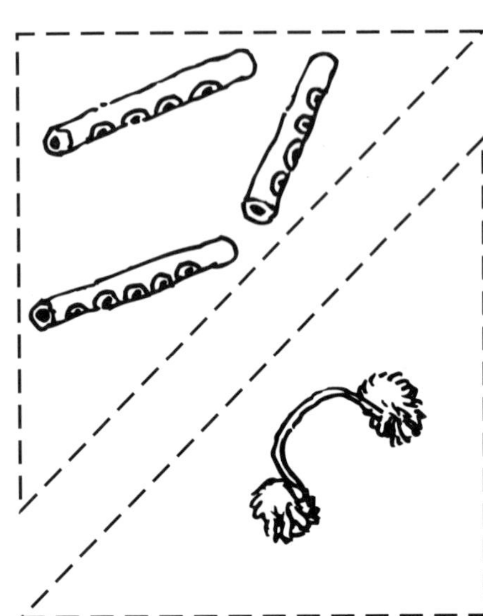

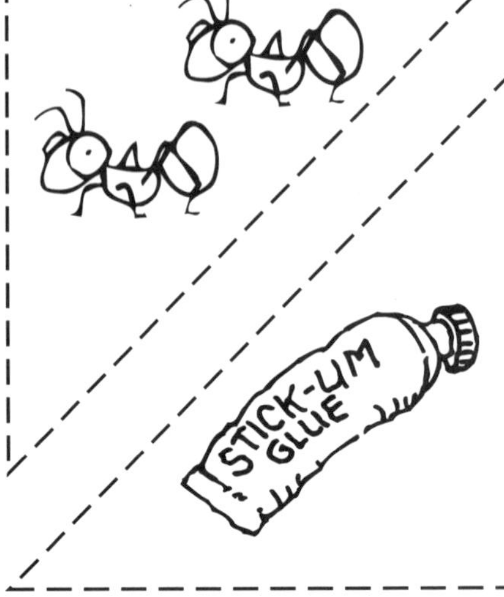

Name ______________________________

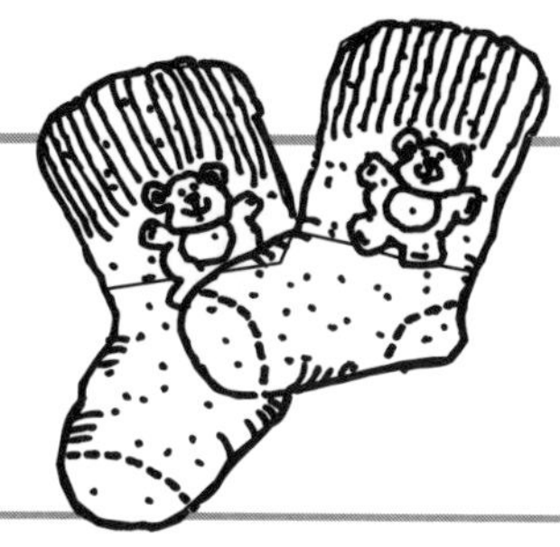

Which Is a Pair?

Is it a pair? Circle **Yes** or **No**.

 Yes No	 Yes No
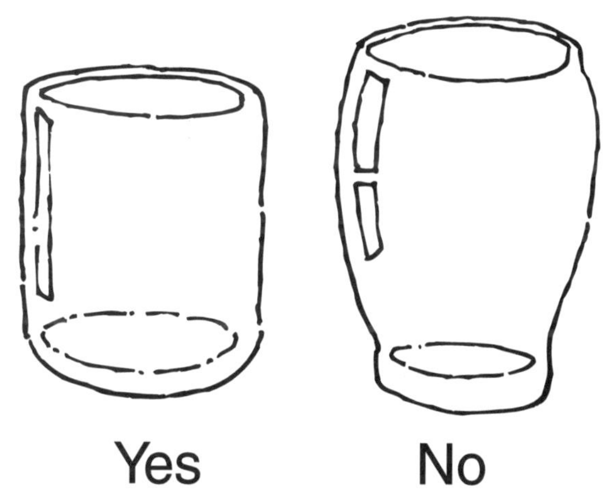 Yes No	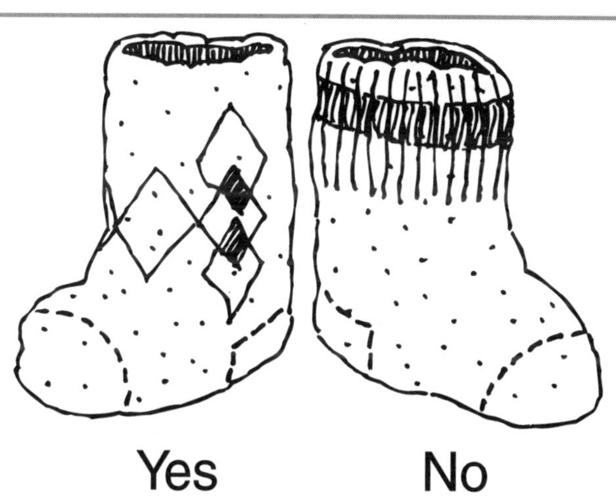 Yes No
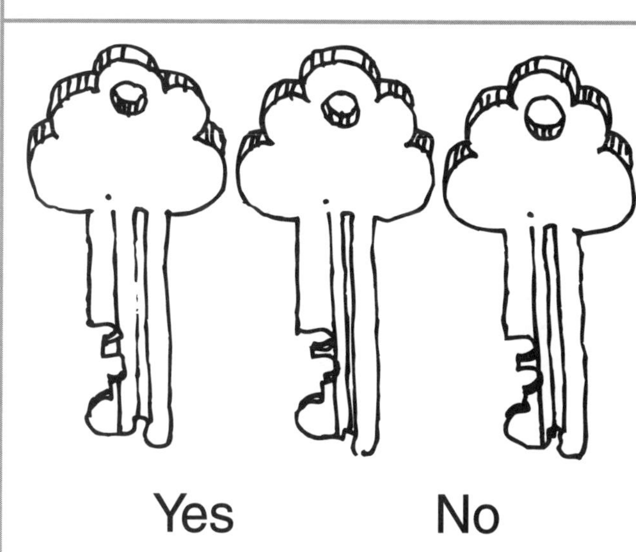 Yes No	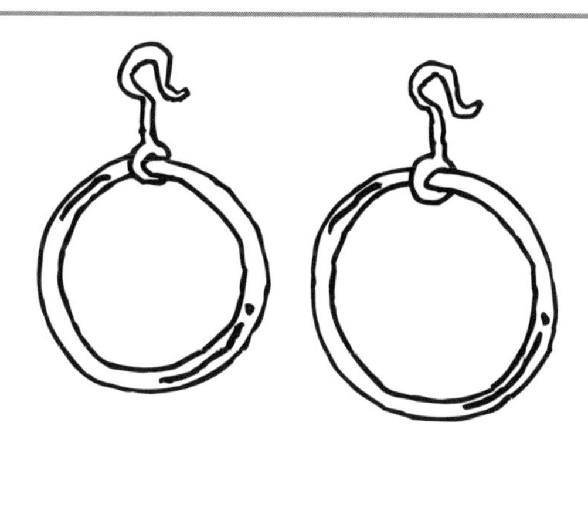 Yes No

Breakfast in Bed

1

Story Dictionary

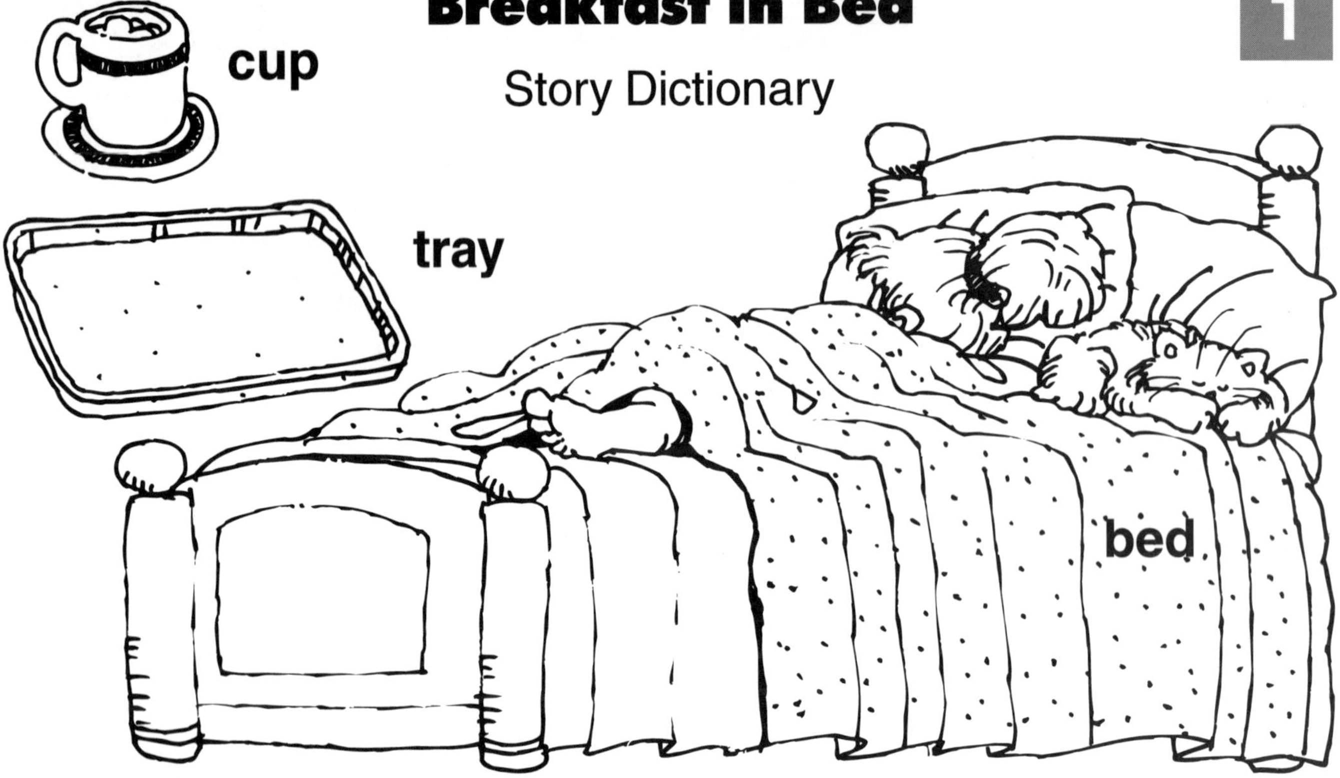

cup

tray

bed

My book:

2

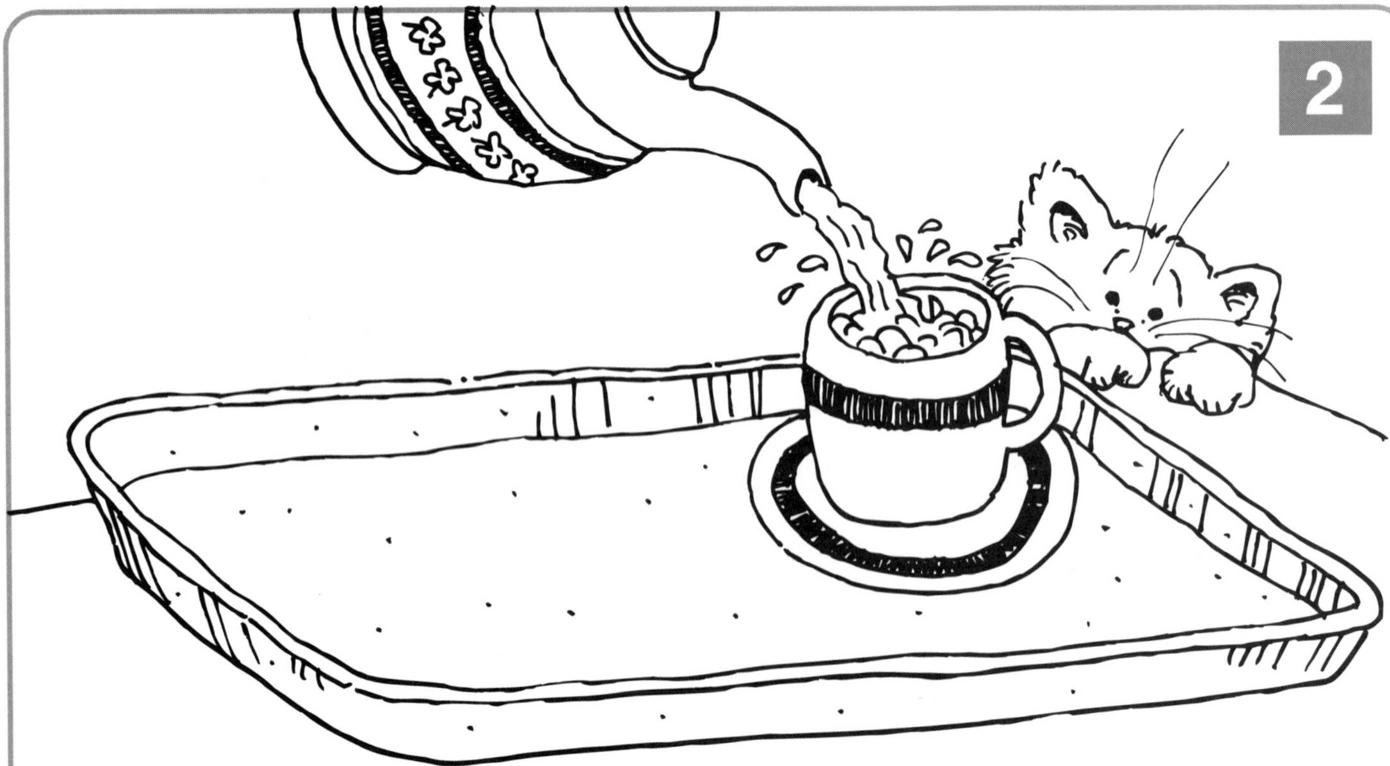

Here's the cup.
Fill it up.

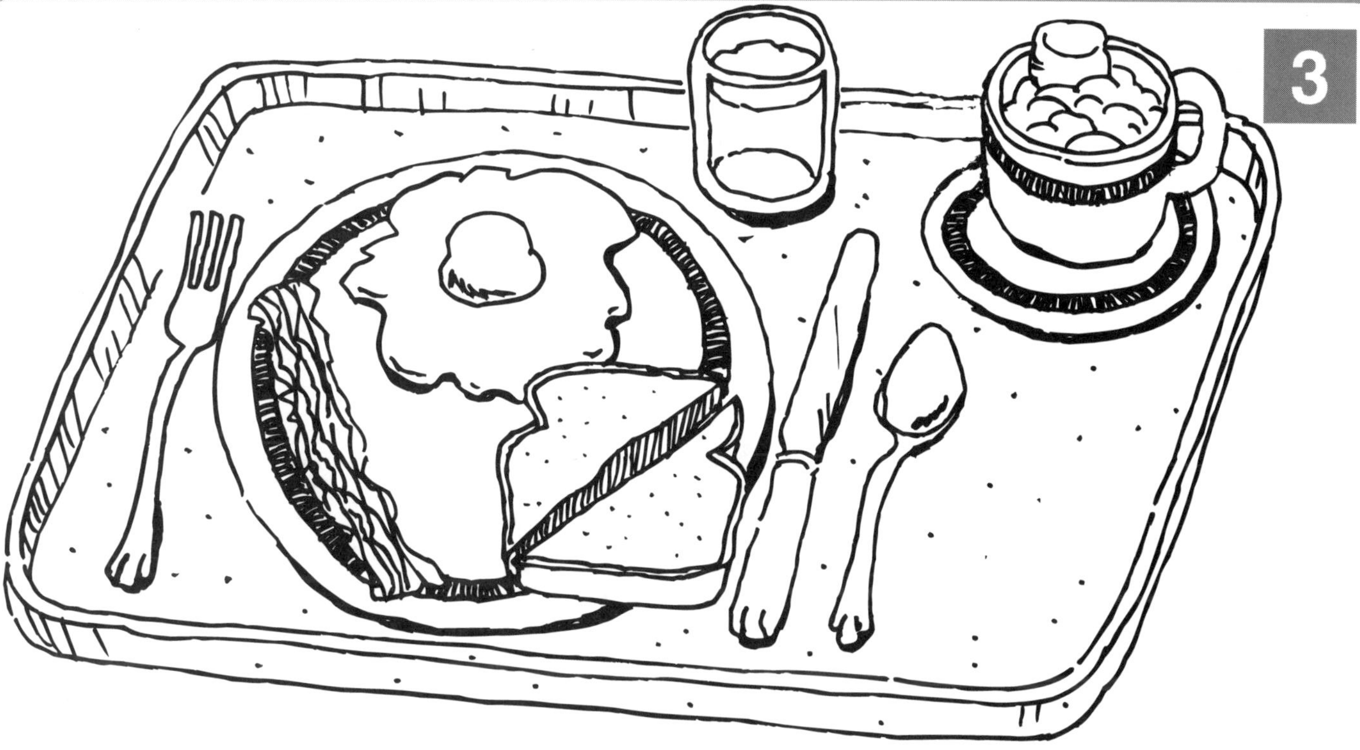

3

Here's the tray.
Take it away.

EMC 745

4

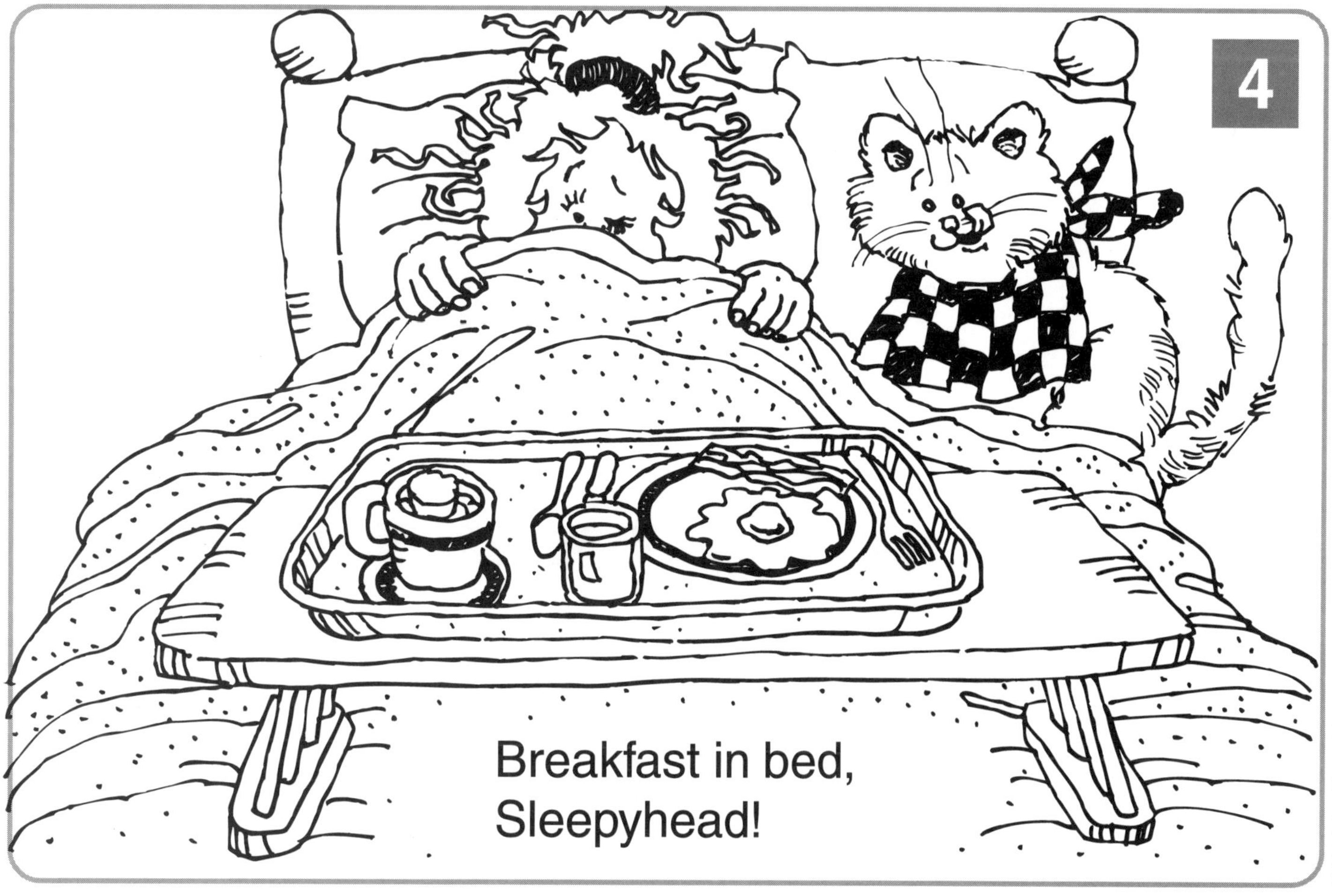

Breakfast in bed,
Sleepyhead!

EMC 745

Name ______________________________

What Did the Story Say?

Number the pictures to show what happened first in the story. Draw your favorite breakfast on the tray.

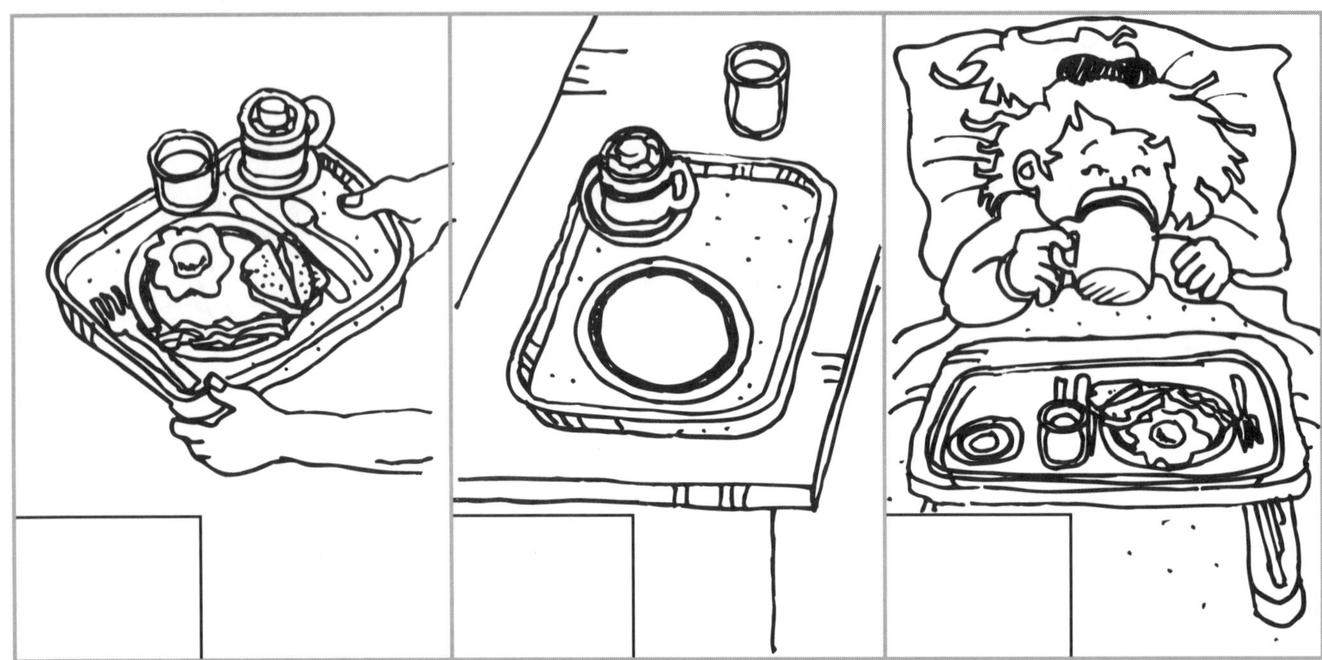

Name ______________________________

Working with Word Families

-ay

Write the words. Cut and paste to show what each word means.

paste pl + ay = ___ ___ ___ ___	paste l + ay = ___ ___ ___	paste sw + ay = ___ ___ ___ ___
paste spr + ay = ___ ___ ___ ___ ___	paste tr + ay = ___ ___ ___ ___	paste p + ay = ___ ___ ___

Write some other **-ay** words here.

____

____

Name ______________________________

What's on the Tray?

Cut and paste to put the things on the right trays.

paste This tray is in the lunchroom.	
paste This tray is in the art room.	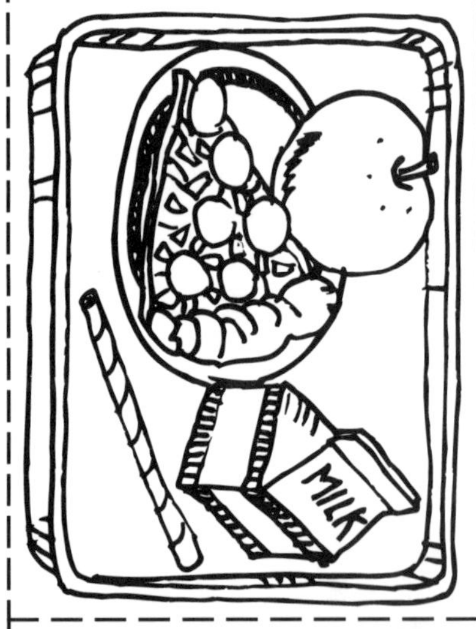
paste This tray is in the nurse's office.	

Name ____________________________

Real or Make-Believe?

Could this be real? Circle **Yes** or **No**.

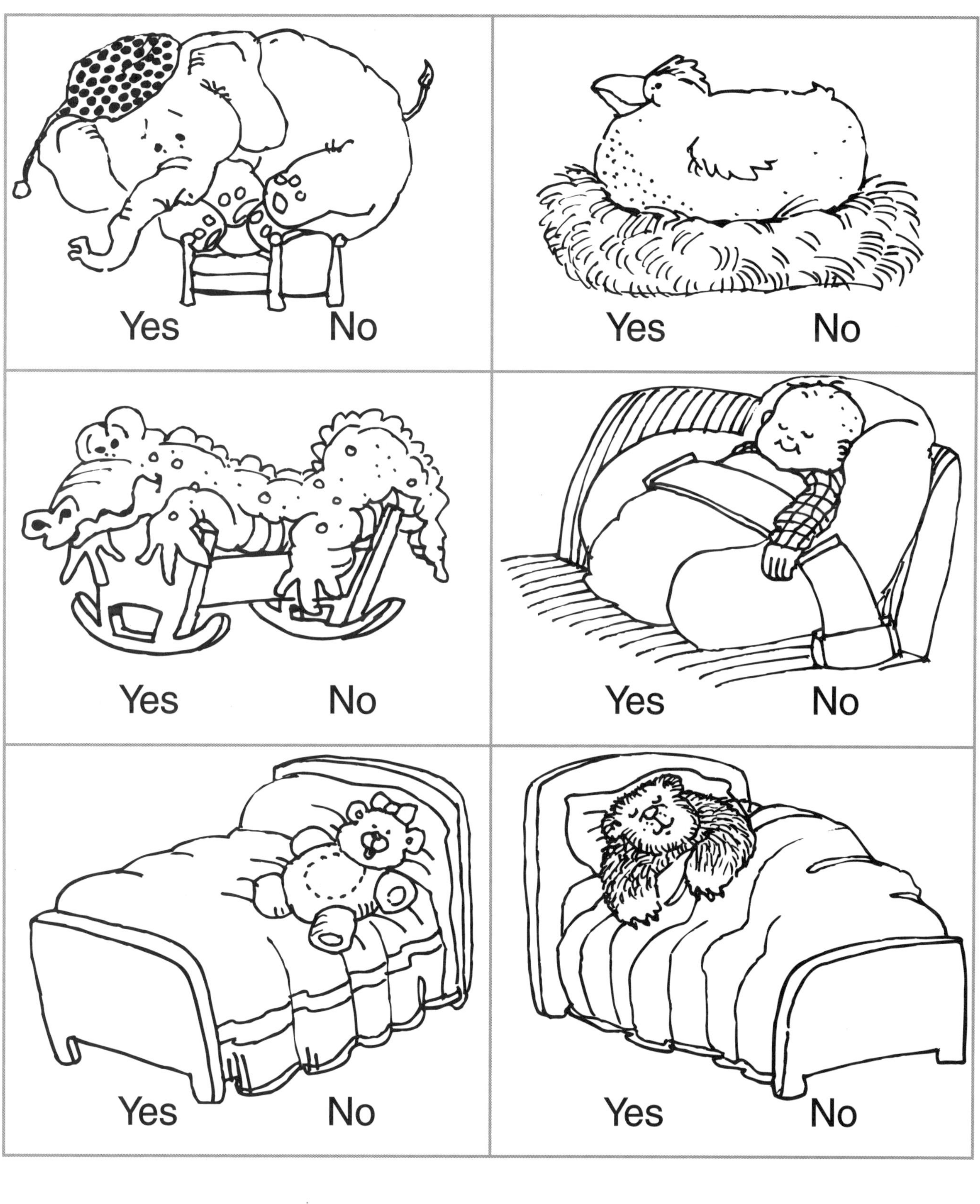

Put It In

Story Dictionary

1

slot

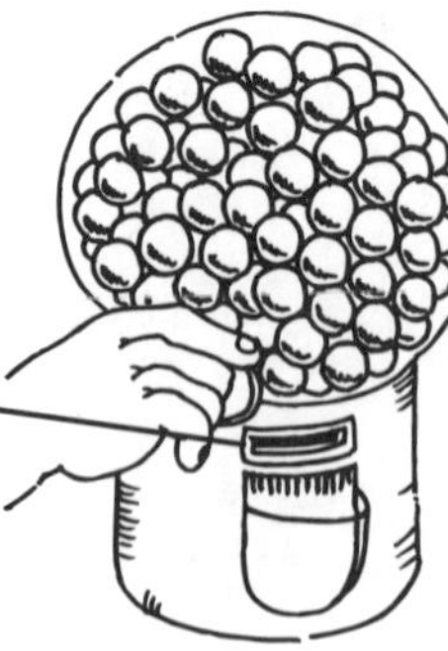

bank

meter

pocket

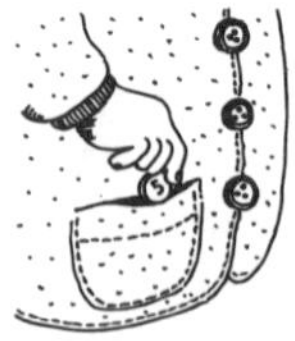

cup

purse

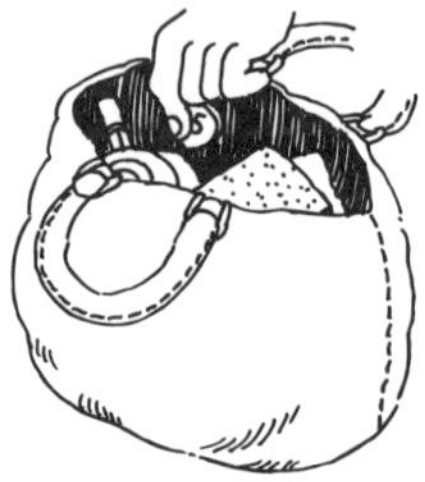

My book:

2

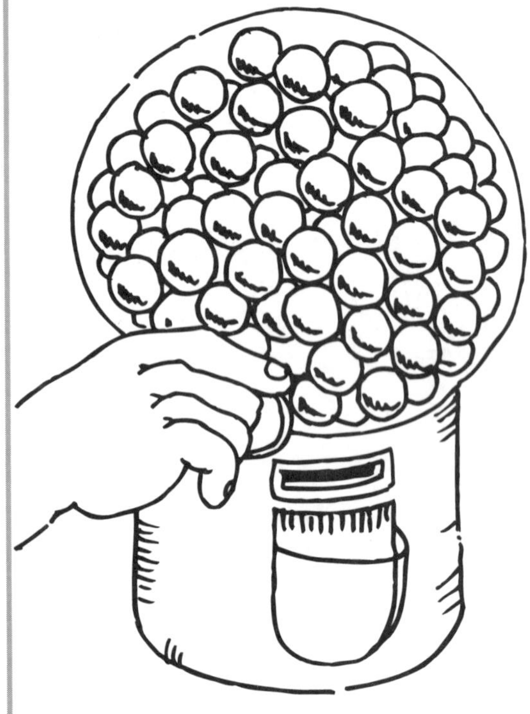

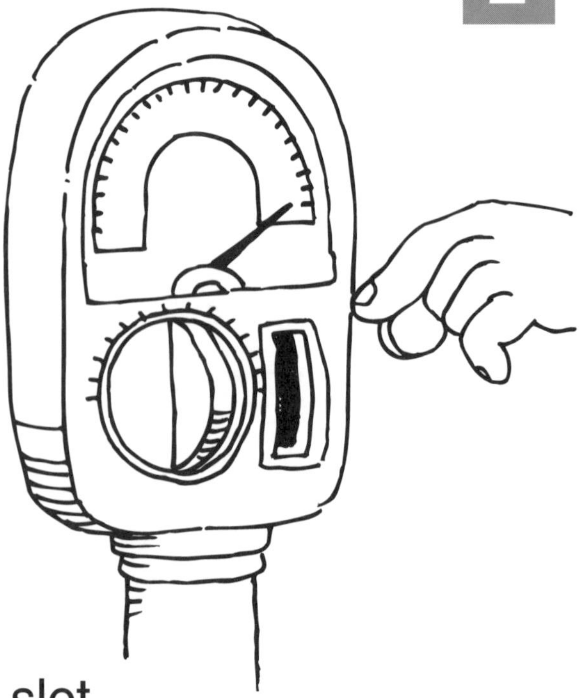

Put a nickel in the slot.
Put a nickel in the meter.

3

Put a nickel in the cup.
Put a nickel in the bank.

  EMC 745

4

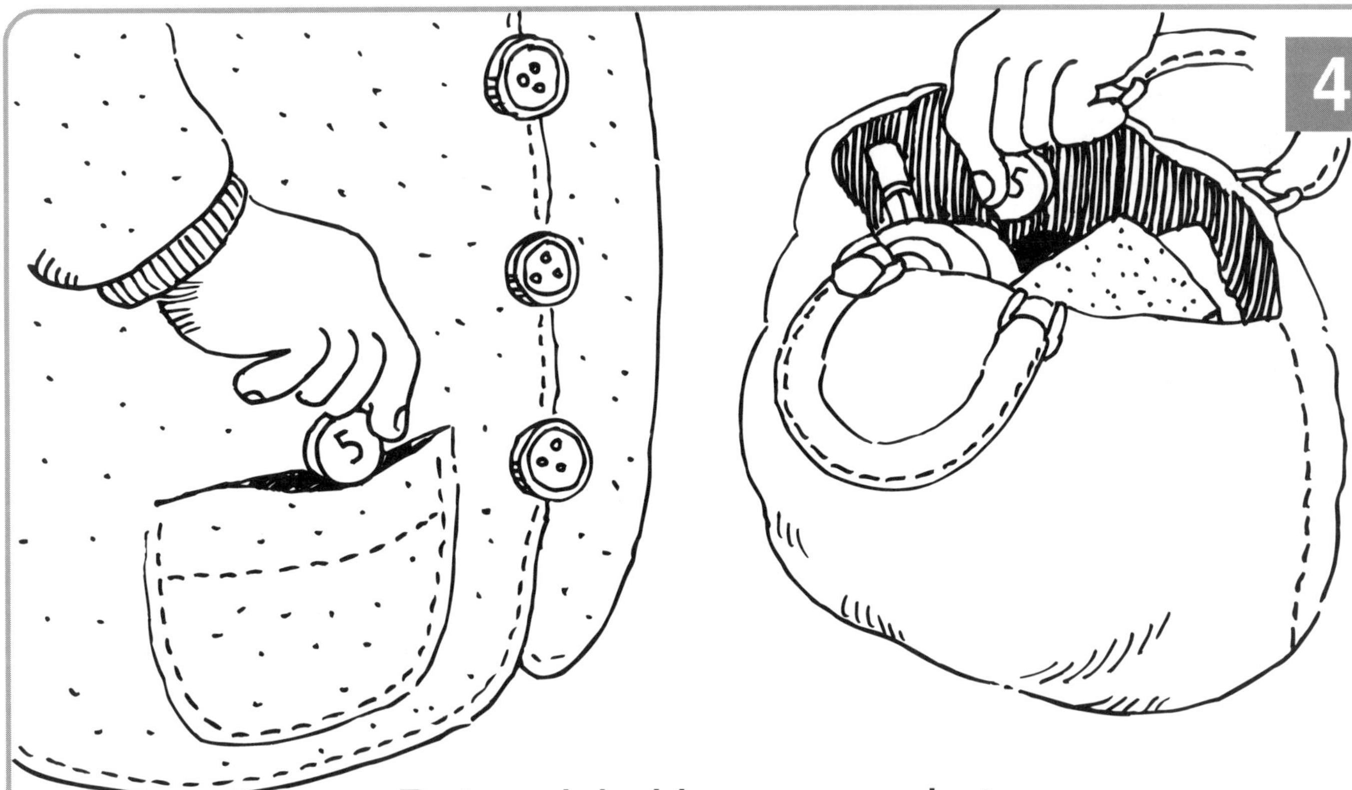

Put a nickel in your pocket.
Put a nickel in your purse.

  EMC 745

Name ____________________________

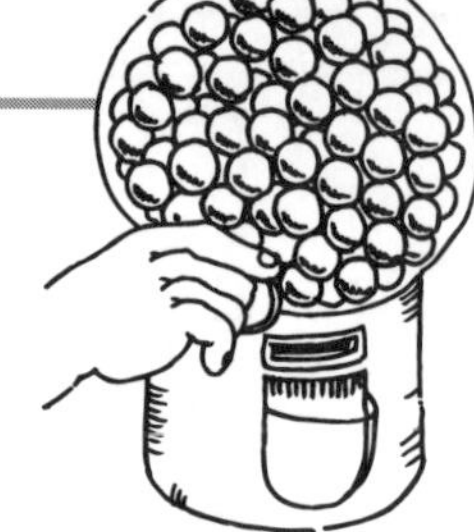

What Did the Story Say?

In the story the children put nickels in six places. Draw them in order here.

1.	2.
3.	4.
5.	6.

Show three places you might put coins.

Name ______________________________

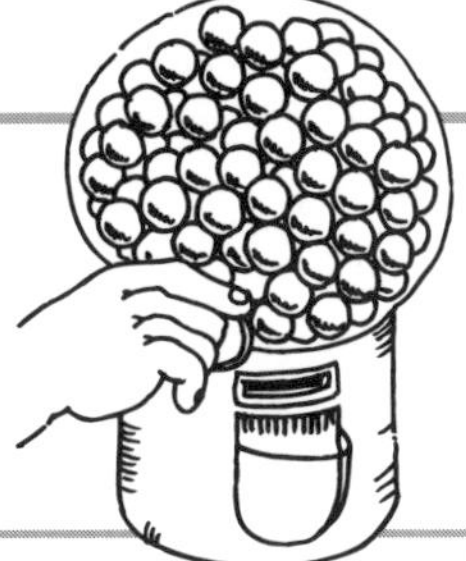

Working with Word Families

-ot

c + ot = ___ ___ ___

n + ot = ___ ___ ___

p + ot = ___ ___ ___

sh + ot = ___ ___ ___ ___

d + ot = ___ ___ ___

tr + ot = ___ ___ ___ ___

Use the words you made to complete these sentences:

A ______________________ is a little circle.

A ______________________ is a little bed.

The man ______________________ an arrow.

The horse can ______________________.

I put the soup in the ______________________.

I am ______________________ going to bed now.

Name ______________________________

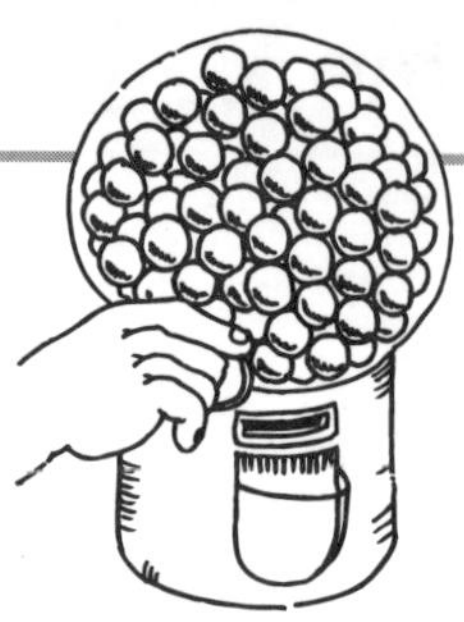

The Sound of *n*

Color the pictures whose names begin with the sound that **n** stands for.

Name ______________________________

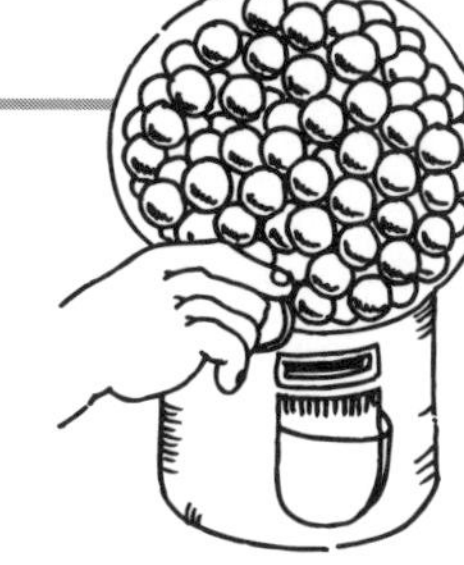

A Place to Keep a Nickel

Connect the dots to draw a place to keep your nickels. Start with 1 and count to 25.

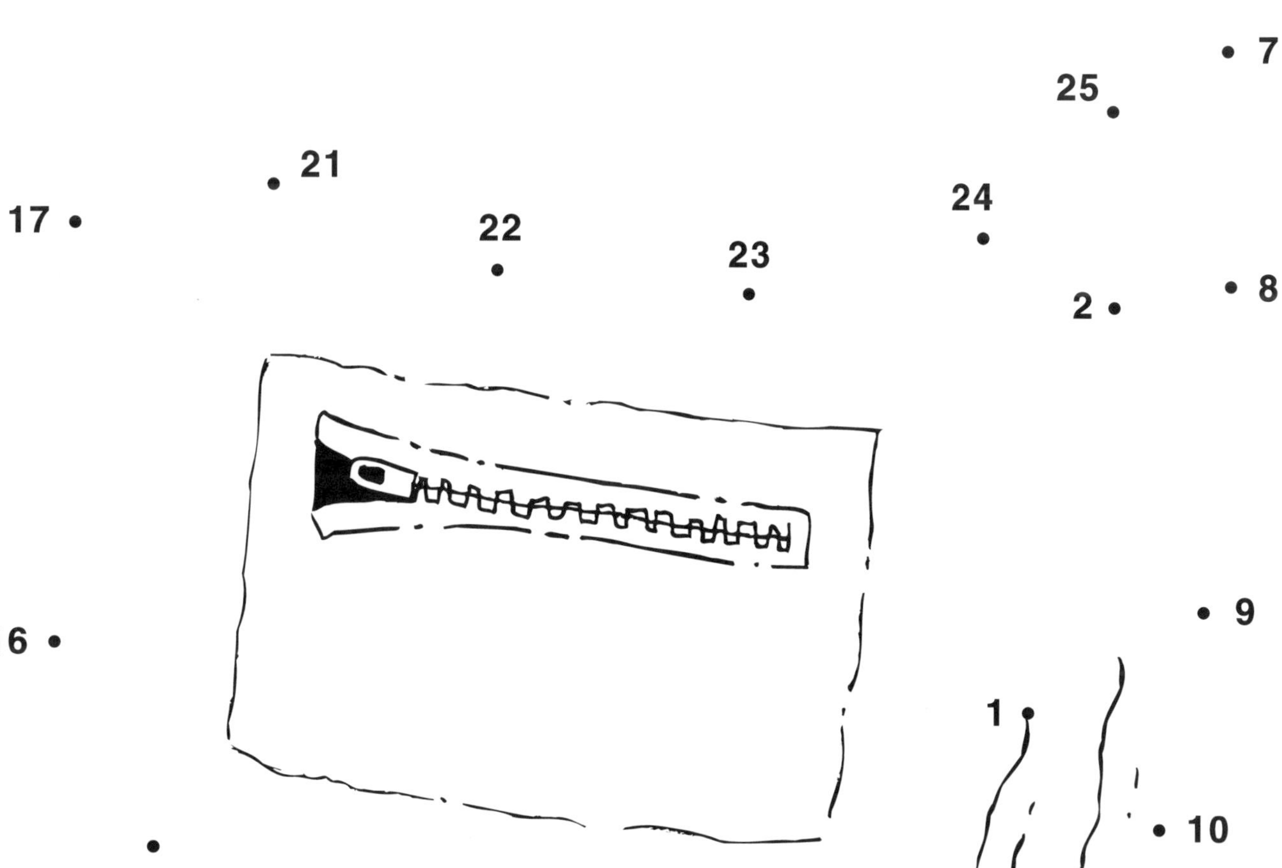

Josh's Bike

Story Dictionary

bike

1

My book:

EMC 745 22 ©1999 by Evan-Moor Corp.

2

Josh's bike is red.

3

Josh's bike is fast.

4

Josh's bike wobbles as it zips past.

23
©1999 by Evan-Moor Corp.

Name ______________________

What Did the Story Say?

Put an **X** on the word that is wrong.
Use a new word. Rewrite the sentence to match the story.

Josh's bike is blue.

____

____

Josh's bike is slow.

____

____

Josh's bike crashes.

____

____

The bike belongs to John.

____

____

Name ______________________________

Working with Word Families

-ike

b + ike = ___ ___ ___ ___

Do you have a bike?

Yes No

l + ike = ___ ___ ___ ___

Write one thing you like.

____

h + ike = ___ ___ ___ ___

Do you like to hike?

Yes No

M + ike = ___ ___ ___ ___

Do you know someone named Mike?

Yes No

tr + ike = ___ ___ ___ ___ ___

Can you ride a trike?

Yes No

Name ______________________________

Following Directions

Read the color words. Color the bike.
Draw a rider. Draw a helmet on the rider's head.

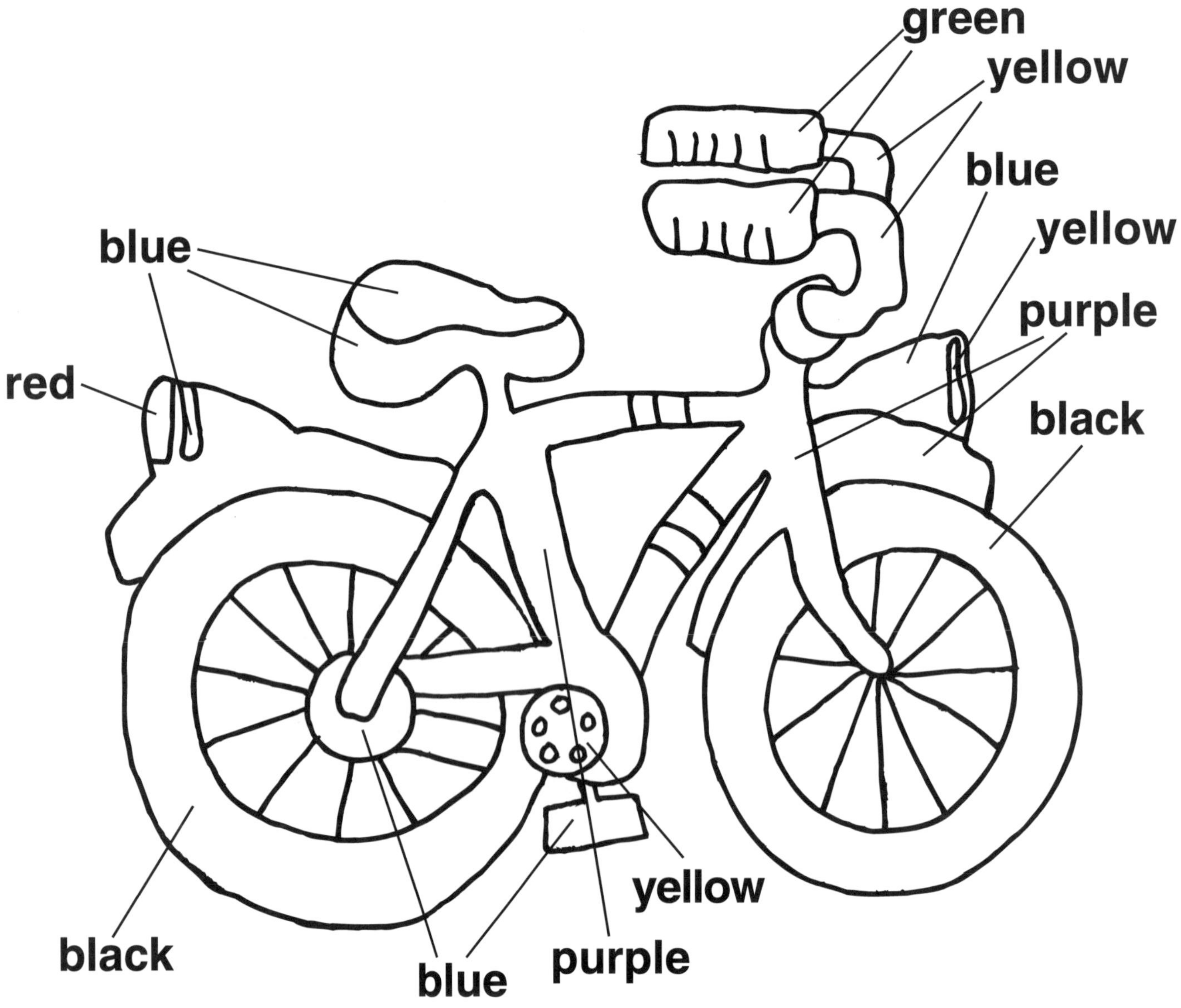

green
yellow
blue
yellow
purple
black
blue
red
black
yellow
purple
blue

Name ______________________________

When It Belongs to Someone

We use **’s** to show that something belongs to someone. The bike belonged to Josh so we say it was Josh’s bike.

Circle the words with **’s**. Finish the sentence to tell what belongs to someone.

The bike’s seat was black.

The seat belongs to the ______________________________.

The boy’s hat was blue.

The hat belongs to the ______________________________.

The jet’s wings were silver.

The wings belong to the ______________________________.

The boy went to his dad’s house.

The house belonged to his ______________________________.

The boy and his dad parked the bikes in the store’s rack.

The rack belonged to the ______________________________.

1

The Egg Search

Story Dictionary

egg

nest

My book:

2

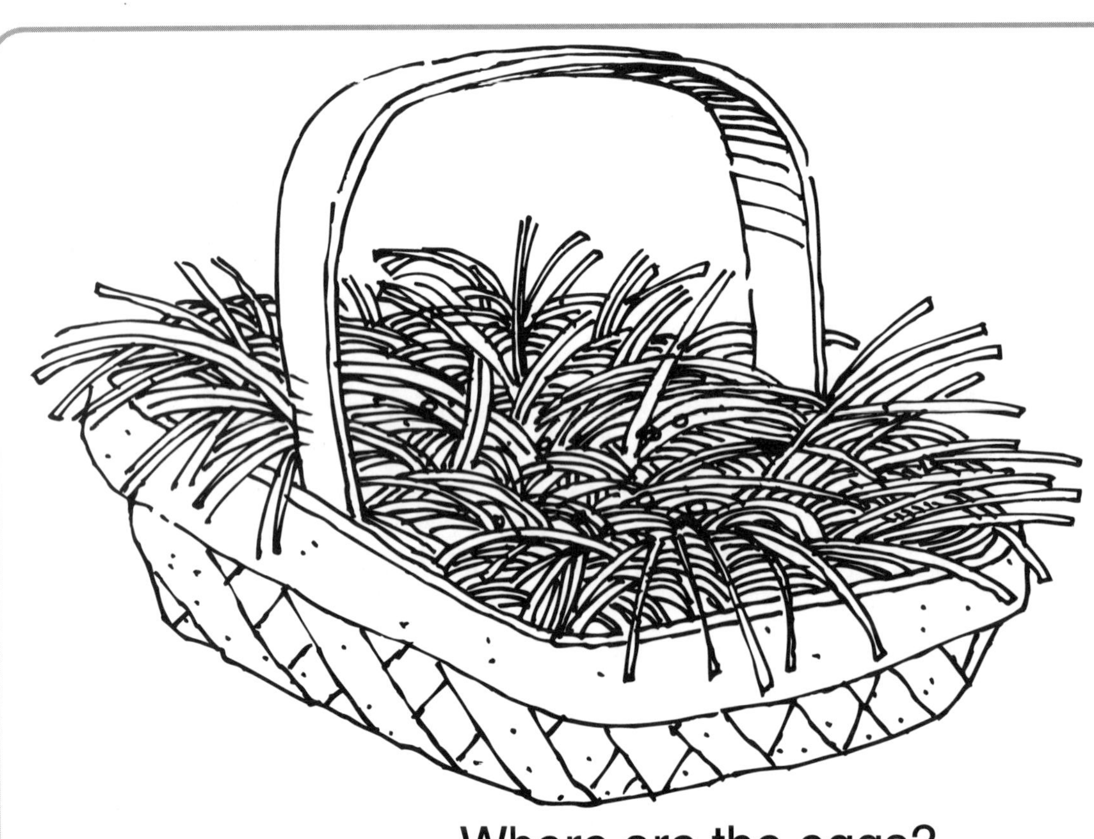

Where are the eggs?

3

Annie, where is your egg?
Peanut, where is your egg?
Butter, where is your egg?

4

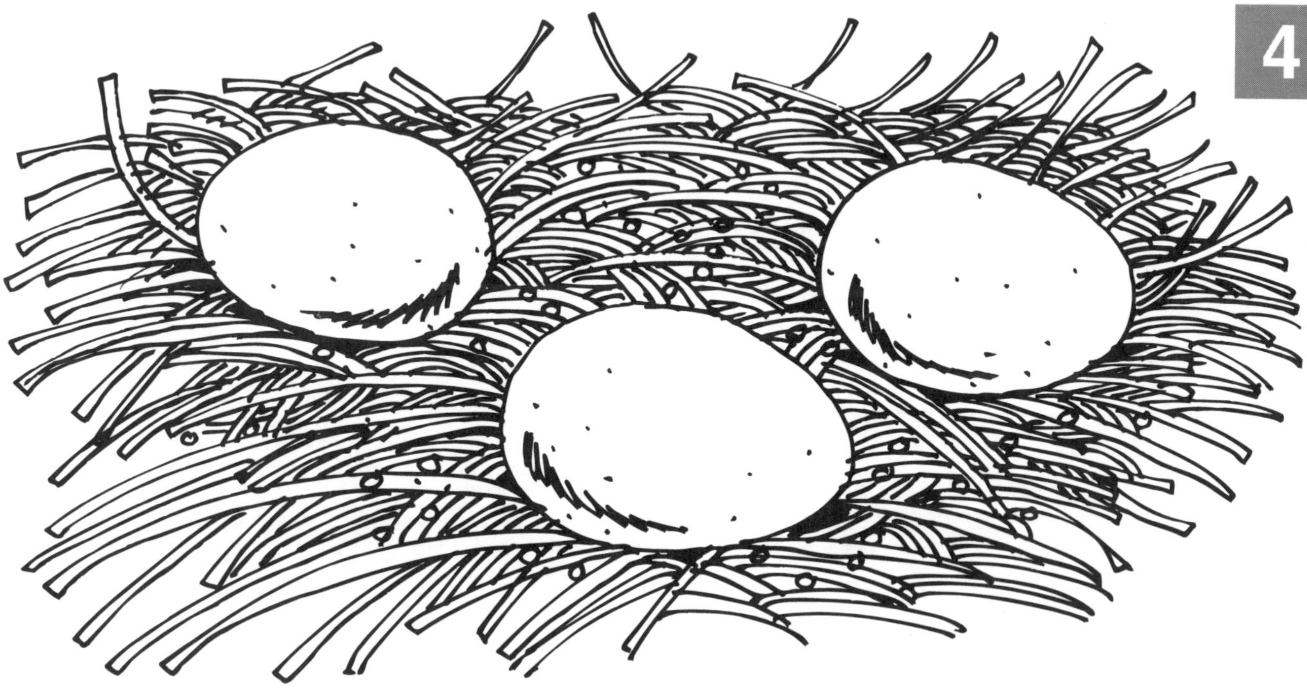

Three hens did their best.
Three eggs in the nest.

Name ______________________

What Did the Story Say?

Draw to show what was in the nest.
Tell about your picture.

Name ______________________________

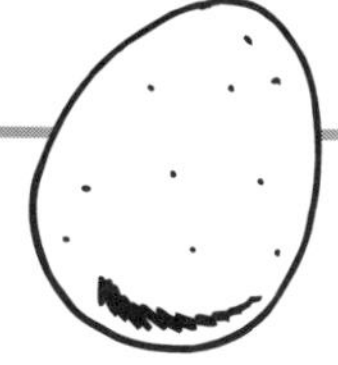

Listening for Sounds

Color the pictures whose names end with the sound that **g** stands for. How many did you find? _____

Name ______________________________

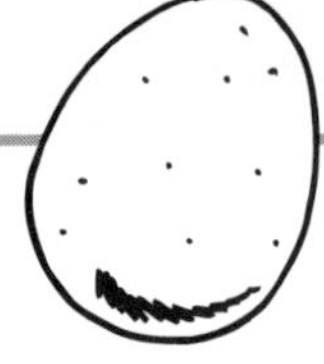

How Do You Like Your Eggs?

Think of all the ways that you like to eat eggs. Mark **Yes** or **No.**

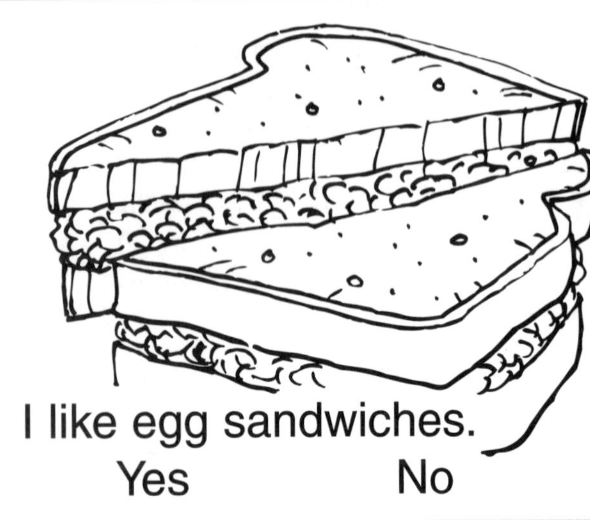

I like egg sandwiches.

Yes No

I like scrambled eggs.

Yes No

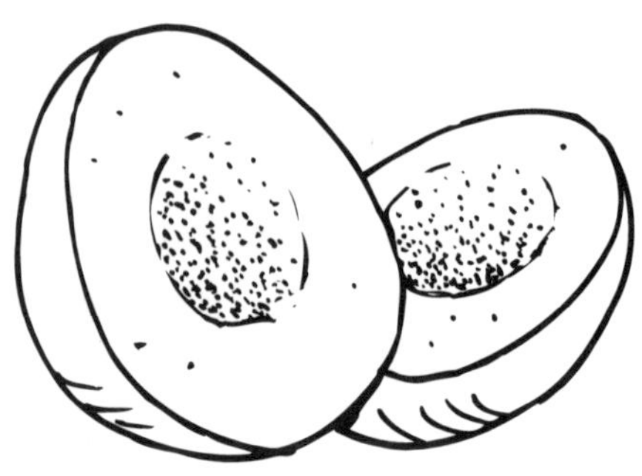

I like hard-boiled eggs.

Yes No

I like fried eggs.

Yes No

Draw your favorite way to eat eggs.

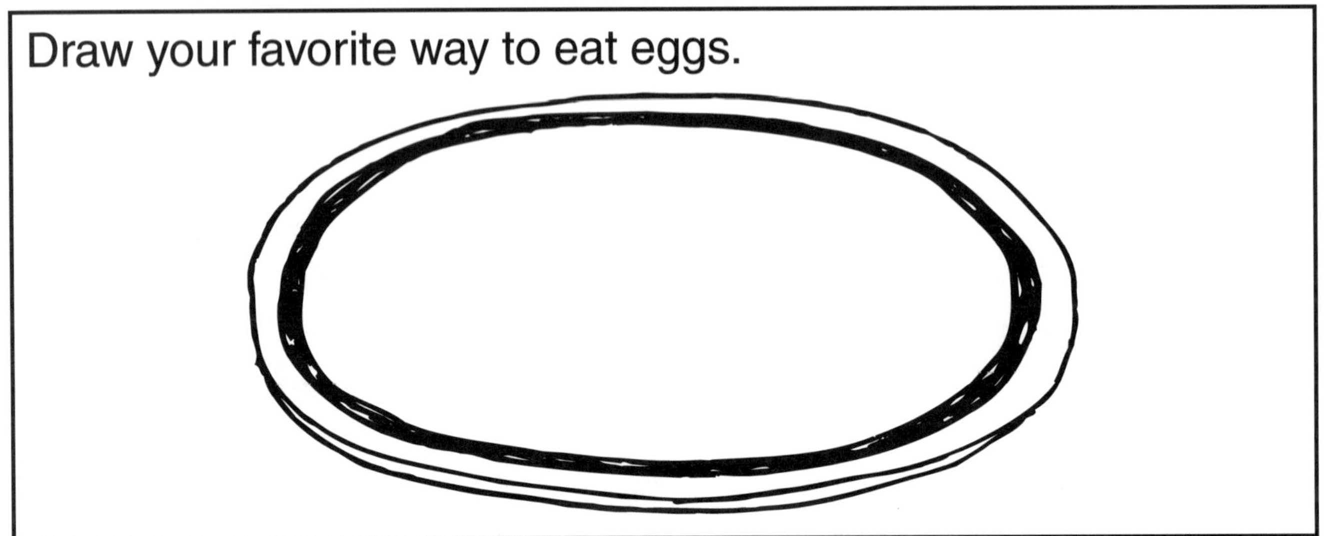

Name ___________________________

Color the Eggs

Read the color words on the eggs. Color to show that you know what each word means.

Draw to show what you think will hatch from the eggs.

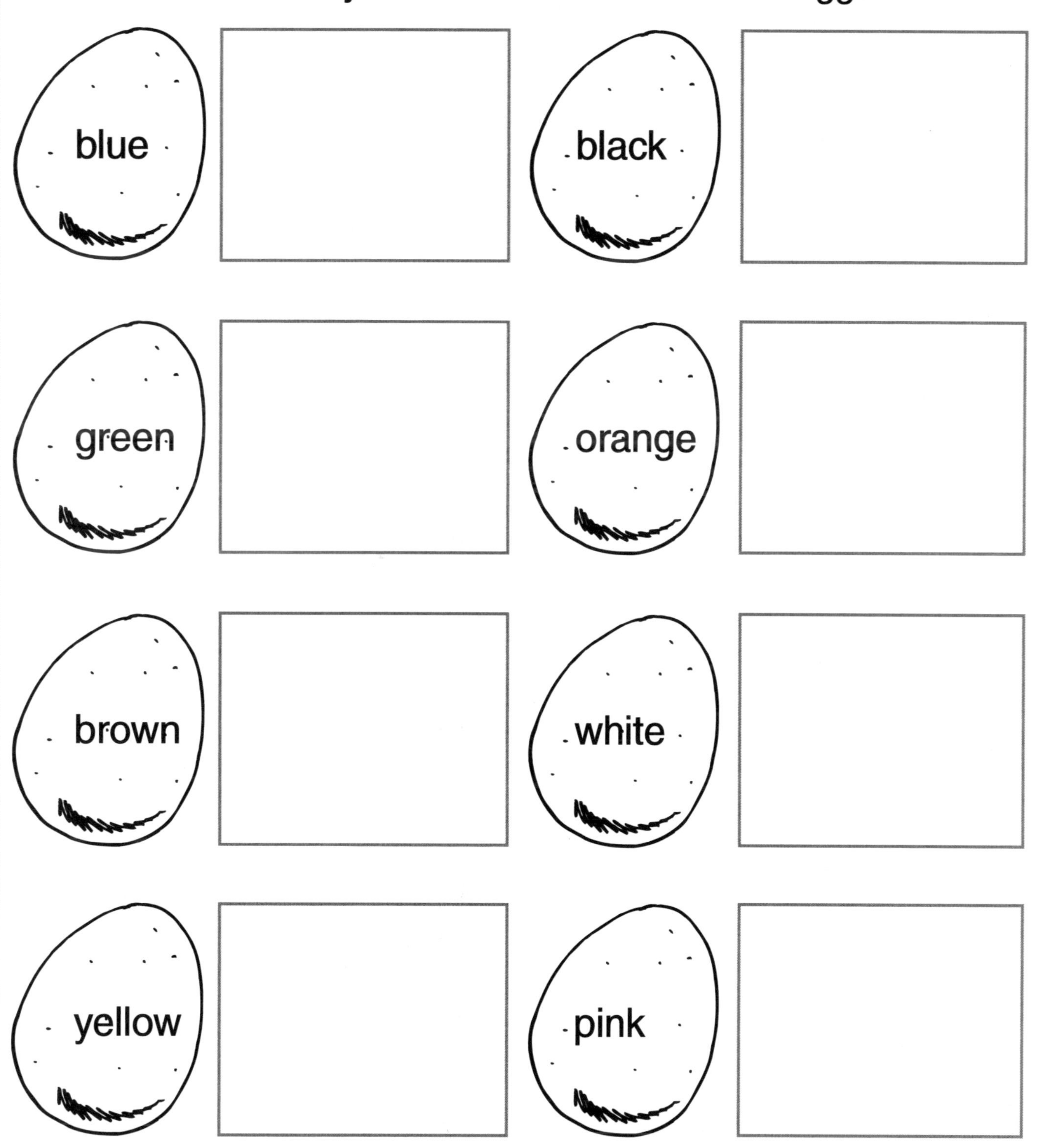

Just Sleeping

1

Story Dictionary

cat

pup

chair

door

boy

My book:

2

One little cat sleeping on the chair.
Waiting for the boy who put him there.

3

One little pup sleeping on the floor
Waiting for the boy to open the door.

EMC 745

4

One little boy sleeping in the bed
While dreams of two friends fill his head.

EMC 745

Name ______________________

What Did the Story Say?

Color, cut, and paste to put the pictures where they belong.

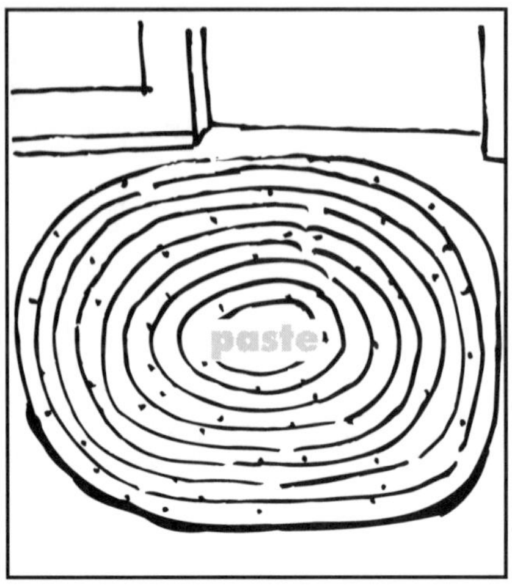

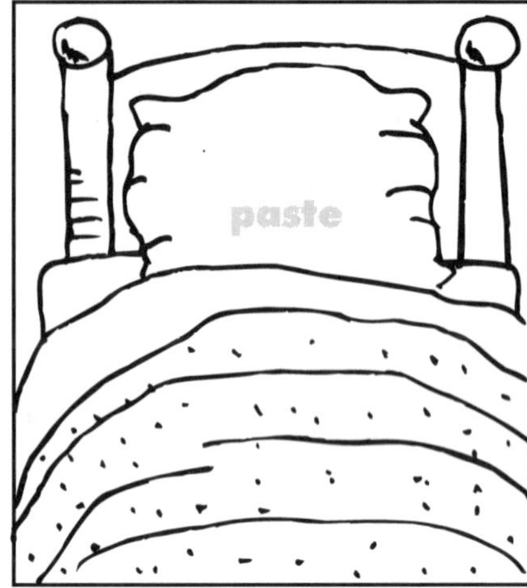

Draw to show what the boy was dreaming about.

Name ______________________

Working with Word Families

-air

h + air = ___ ___ ___ ___

Draw a man with lots of hair.

Draw a man with a little hair.

ch + air = ___ ___ ___ ___ ___

Draw a high chair.

Draw a soft chair.

p + air =

___ ___ ___ ___

st + air =

___ ___ ___ ___ ___

Draw a pair on the stair.

Name ____________________

My Friends

Draw two of your friends.

Write to tell what they are doing.

Name ______________________

More Than One Word

Read the sentences. Circle the words that tell about sleeping. Then color the pictures.

 The baby is napping.	 Daddy snoozes in his chair.
 The bear hibernates inside the cave.	 Grandma dozes in the rocker.

Strike Up the Band

1

Story Dictionary

flute

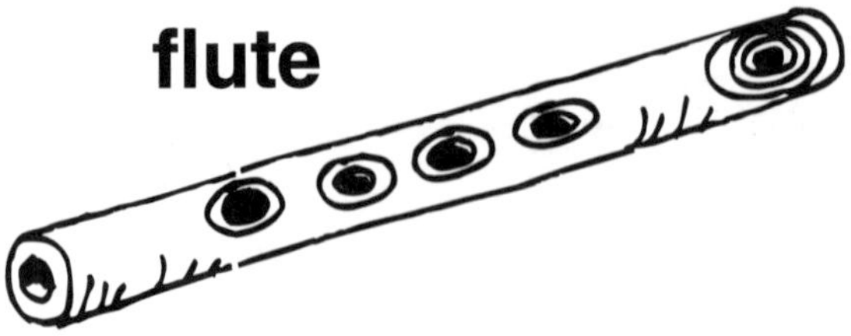

drum

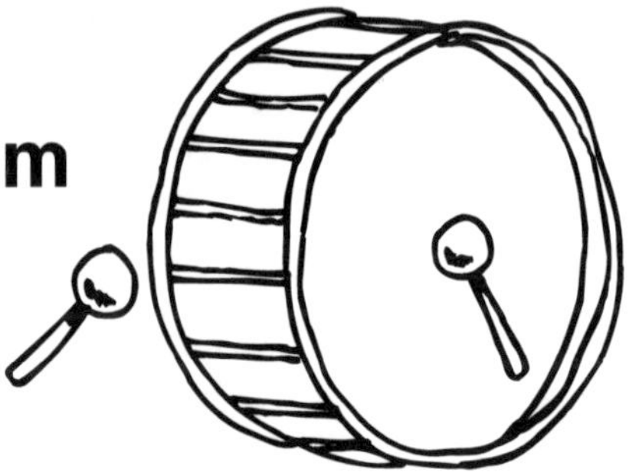

band

My book:

2

Blow the flute.
To-toot-tee-toot

3

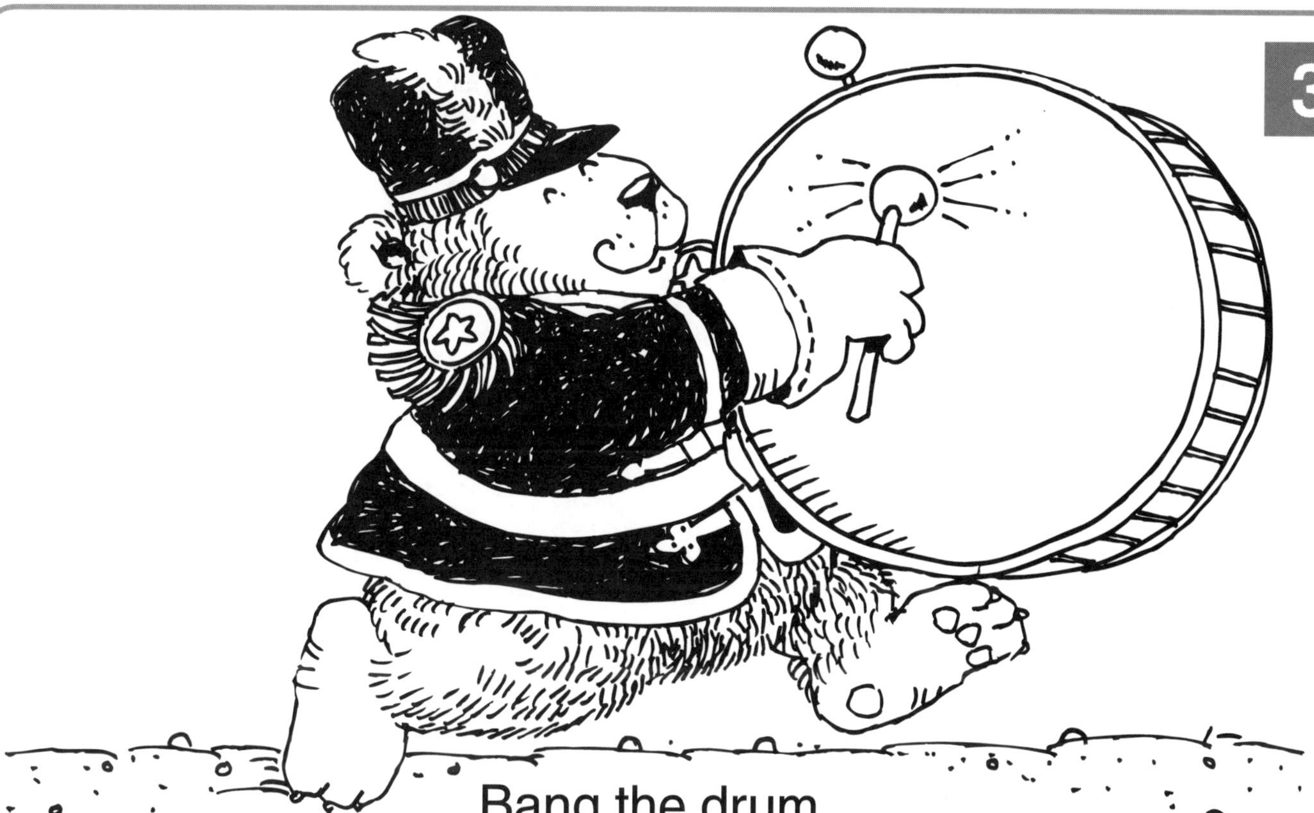

Bang the drum.
Rum-tum-tee-tum

  EMC 745

4

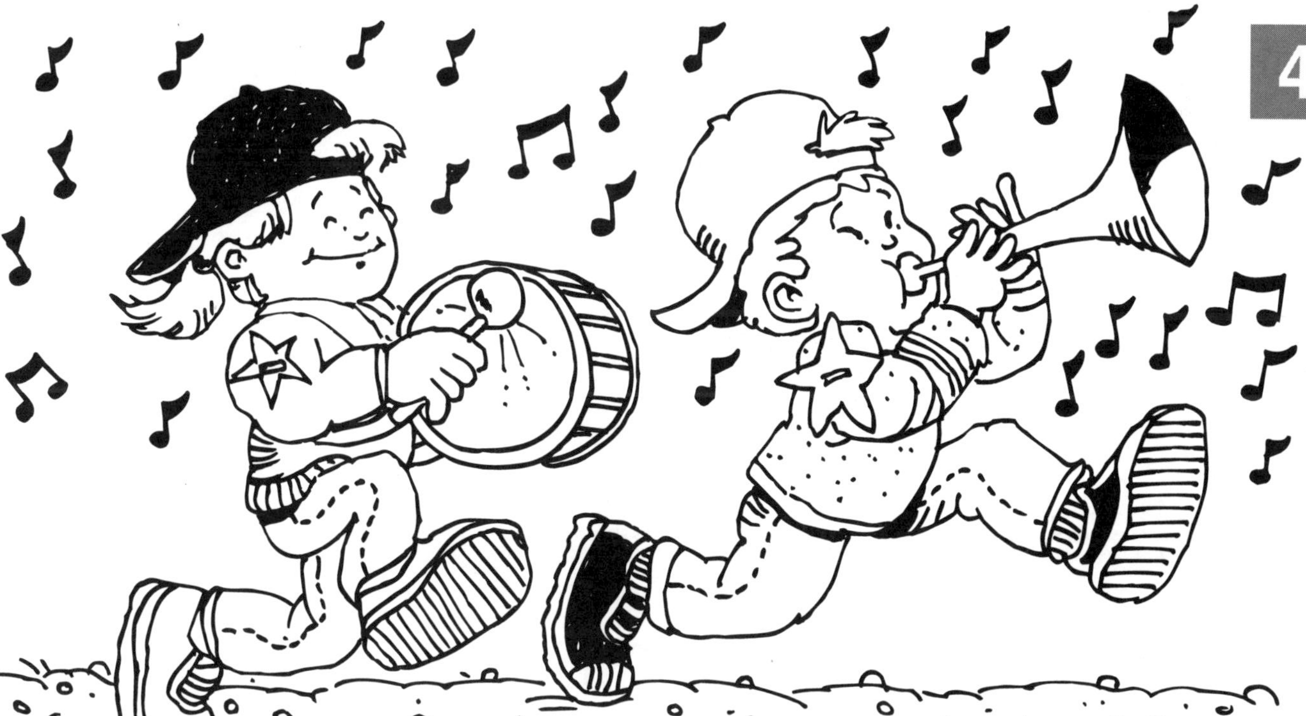

Join the band.
Won't it be grand!

  EMC 745

Name ______________________________

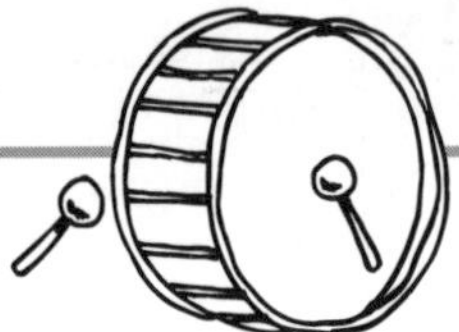

What Did the Story Say?

Circle the word that answers each question correctly.

What do you do to a flute? blow bang join 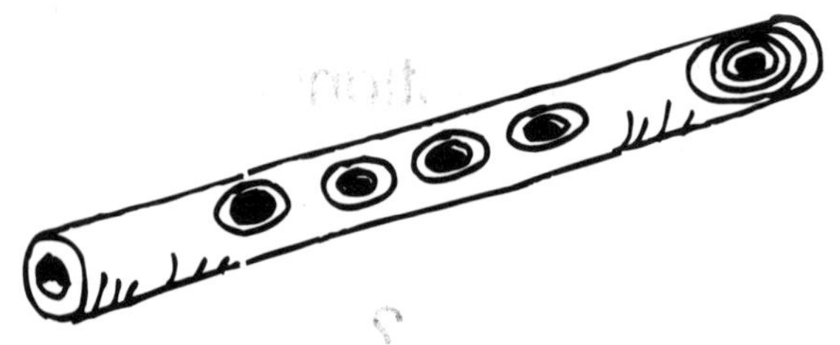	What do you do to a drum? blow bang join 
How do you get in a band? blow bang join 	Draw an instrument that you would like to play. Tell about its sound.

Name ____________________

Working with Word Families

-and

b + and =	s + and =
___ ___ ___ ___	___ ___ ___ ___
h + and =	gr + and =
___ ___ ___ ___	___ ___ ___ ___ ___
l + and =	st + and =
___ ___ ___ ___	___ ___ ___ ___ ___

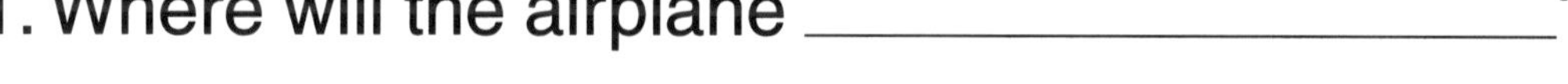

Use the words you made to complete these questions. Then write an answer.

1. Where will the airplane ____________?

____

____

2. Which ____________ do you write with?

____

____

3. Do you like to dig in the ____________?

____

____

Name ______________________________

The Sound of *b*

Color the pictures whose names begin with the sound that **b** stands for.

Name ____________________

Strike Up the Band!

Color the instrument. Answer the question.

Hear the flute.  I like its sound. Yes No	Hear the drum. 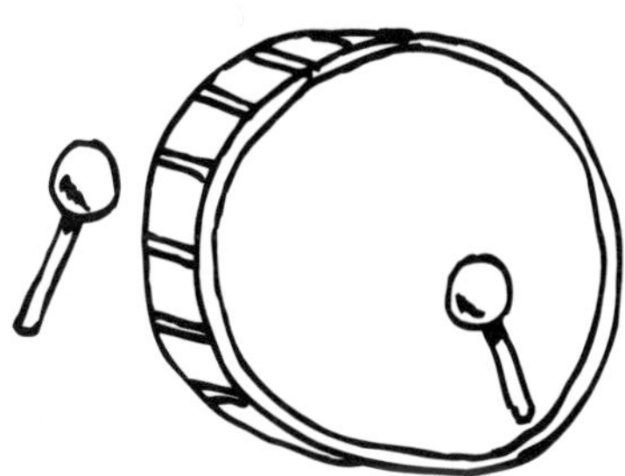 I like its sound. Yes No
Hear the horn. 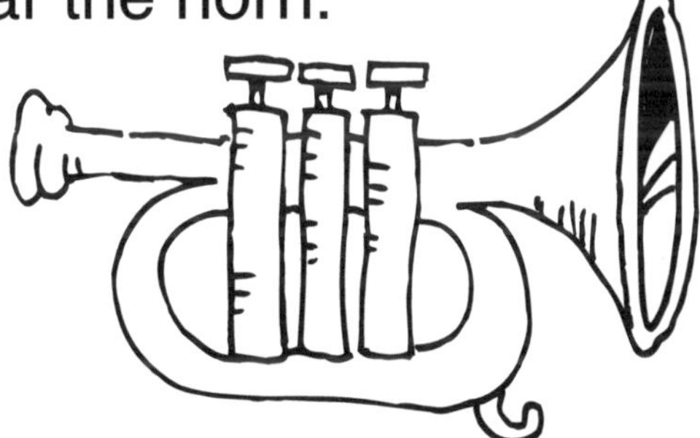 I like its sound. Yes No	Hear the sax. 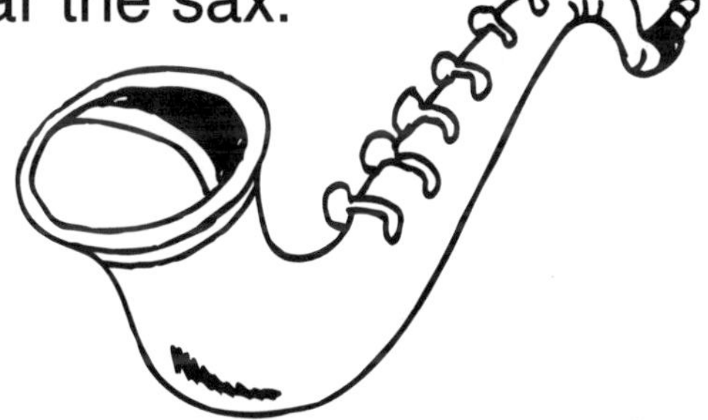 I like its sound. Yes No
Hear the piano.  I like its sound. Yes No	Hear the triangle. 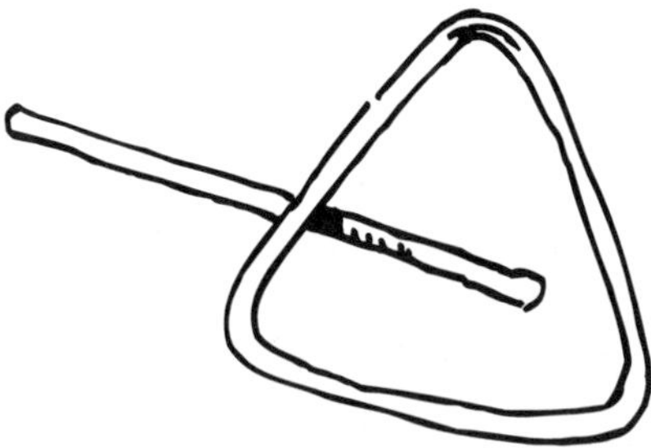 I like its sound. Yes No

My Puppy Snickers

1

Story Dictionary

door

Snickers

kibble

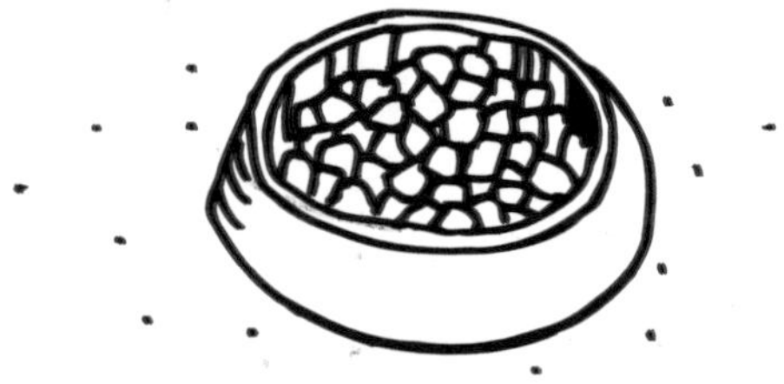

lap

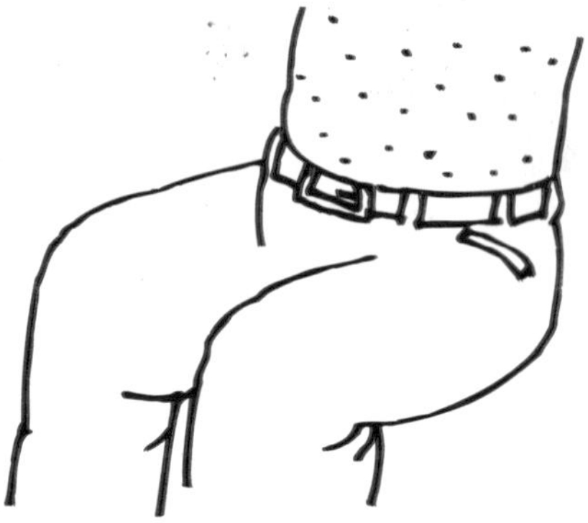

My book:

2

Snickers loves to explore.
He meets me at the door.

3

Snickers loves to nibble.
He eats up all his kibble.

4

Snickers loves to dognap.
He snuggles on my lap.

Name ______________________________

What Did the Story Say?

Write and draw to show three things that Snickers loves to do.

1.

2.

3.

Write and draw to show something else that Snickers might like to do.

Name ______________________________

Working with Word Families

-ap

Color, cut, and paste to show what each word means.

paste n + ap = ___ ___ ___	paste l + ap = ___ ___ ___	paste cl + ap = ___ ___ ___ ___
paste str + ap = ___ ___ ___ ___ ___	paste c + ap = ___ ___ ___	paste m + ap = ___ ___ ___

Write some other **-ap** words here.

____

____

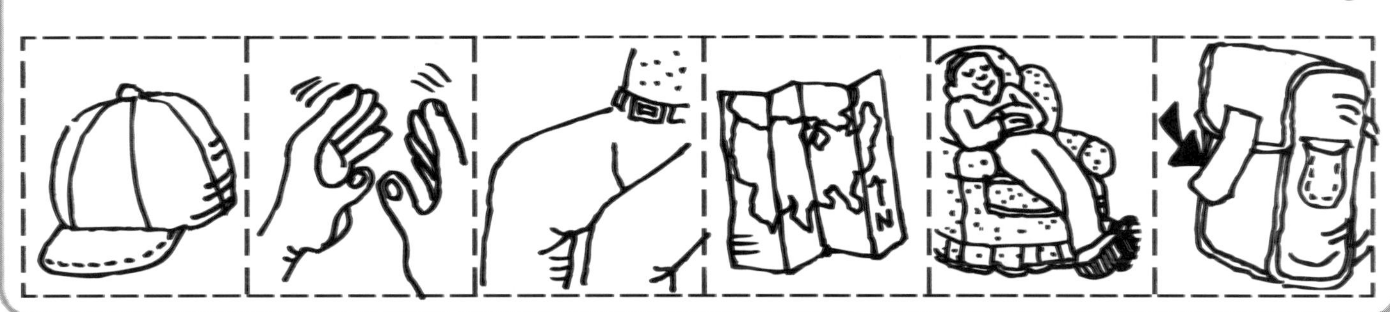

Name ______________________________

New Words for Naps

A catnap is a short nap. Someone made up the word because many cats take short naps. Draw a picture to show who is napping. Write a sentence using each new word.

grandpanap	bearnap
______________________ ______________________ ______________________	______________________ ______________________ ______________________
bugnap	**turtlenap**
______________________ ______________________ ______________________	______________________ ______________________ ______________________

Name ____________________

Words That Tell Where

Use the words to complete these sentences.

The car goes ____________________.

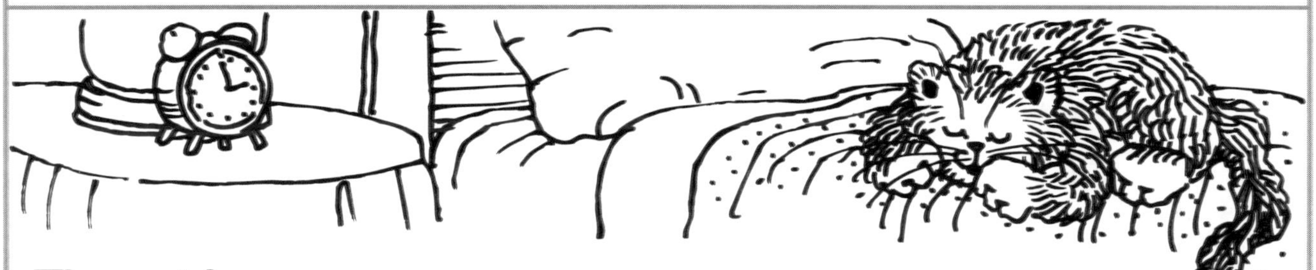

The cat is ____________________.

The man is ____________________.

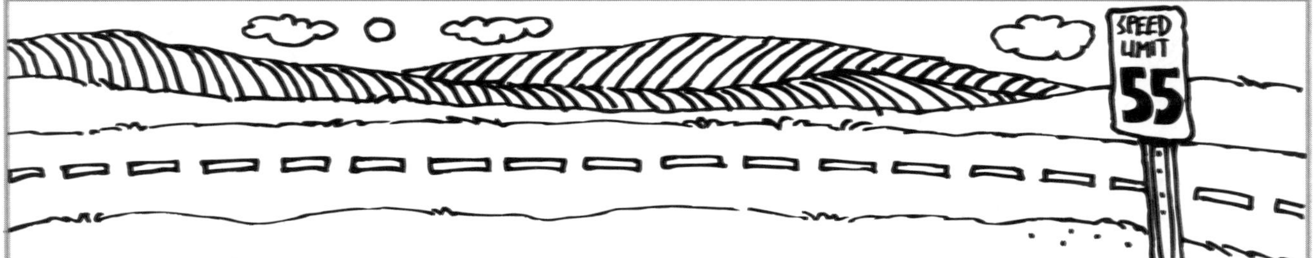

The sign is ____________________.

Word Box

at the door	over the hill
by the road	on the bed

Isn't It?

1

Story Dictionary

pretty

funny

great

My book:

2

Oh, isn't it pretty?

I can't see!

3

Gosh, isn't it great?

I can't see!

4

Ooo, isn't it funny?
It's as funny as can be!

EMC 745

53

©1999 by Evan-Moor Corp.

Name ____________________

What Did the Story Say?

What was the problem?

____

____

How was it solved?

____

____

Draw to show the three things in the parade.

Name ______________________

Working with Word Families

-ee

kn + ee = ___ ___ ___ ___ Draw a knee.	fr + ee = ___ ___ ___ ___ Draw something that is free.
thr + ee = ___ ___ ___ ___ ___ b + ee = ___ ___ ___ tr + ee = ___ ___ ___ ___	Draw three bees buzzing by a tree.

Name ____________________

Contractions

A contraction is a short way to write two words.
We use an apostrophe to show there are missing letters.

Write the letters that are missing in each contraction.

is + not = isn't ☐

can + not = can't ☐ ☐

it + is = it's ☐

Write two sentences using each contraction.

1. ____

____

2. ____

____

3. ____

____

Name ______________________

Questions and Answers

Write a sentence to answer the questions.

What did you see on the way to school?

____

What did you do last night?

____

What did you eat for supper?

____

Write your own question. Have a friend write the answer.

____

____

____

____

____

____

Mr. Scarecrow

1

Story Dictionary

head

hat

shirt

pants

My book:

EMC 745

2

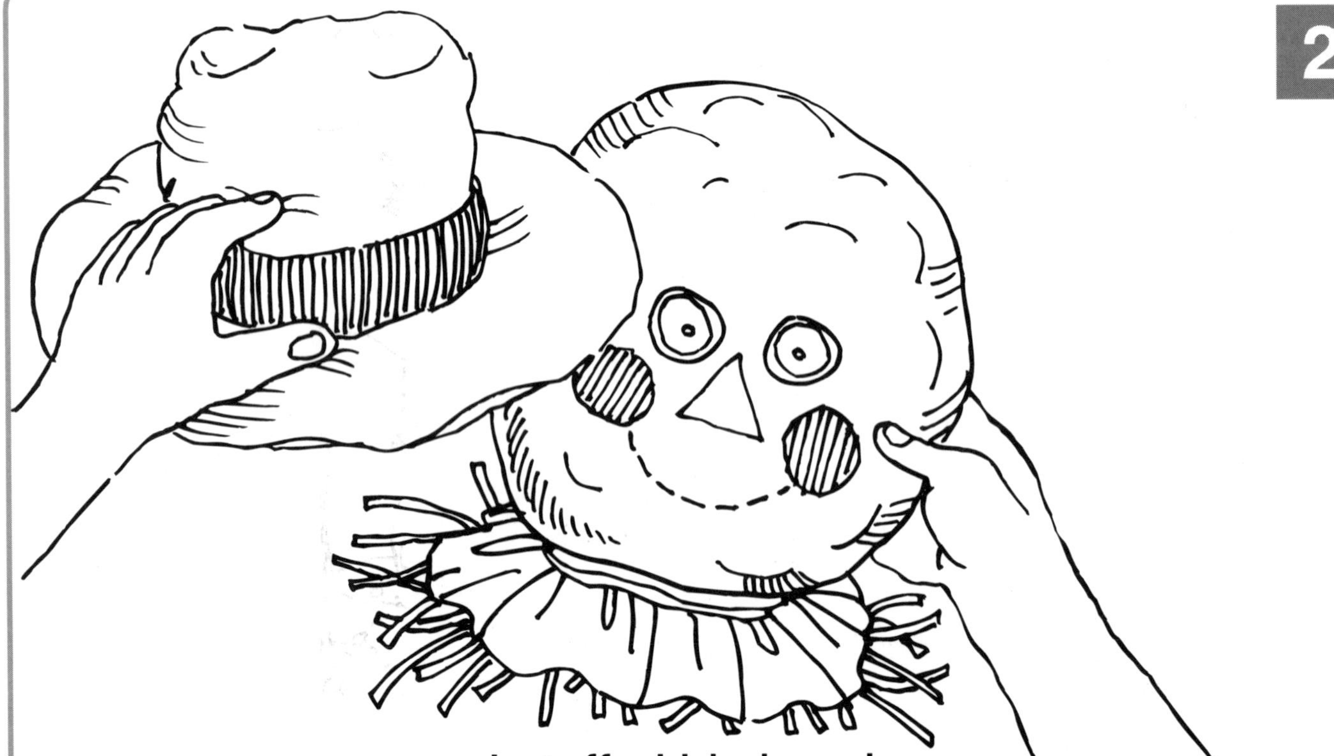

I stuffed his head.
And put on his hat.

EMC 745

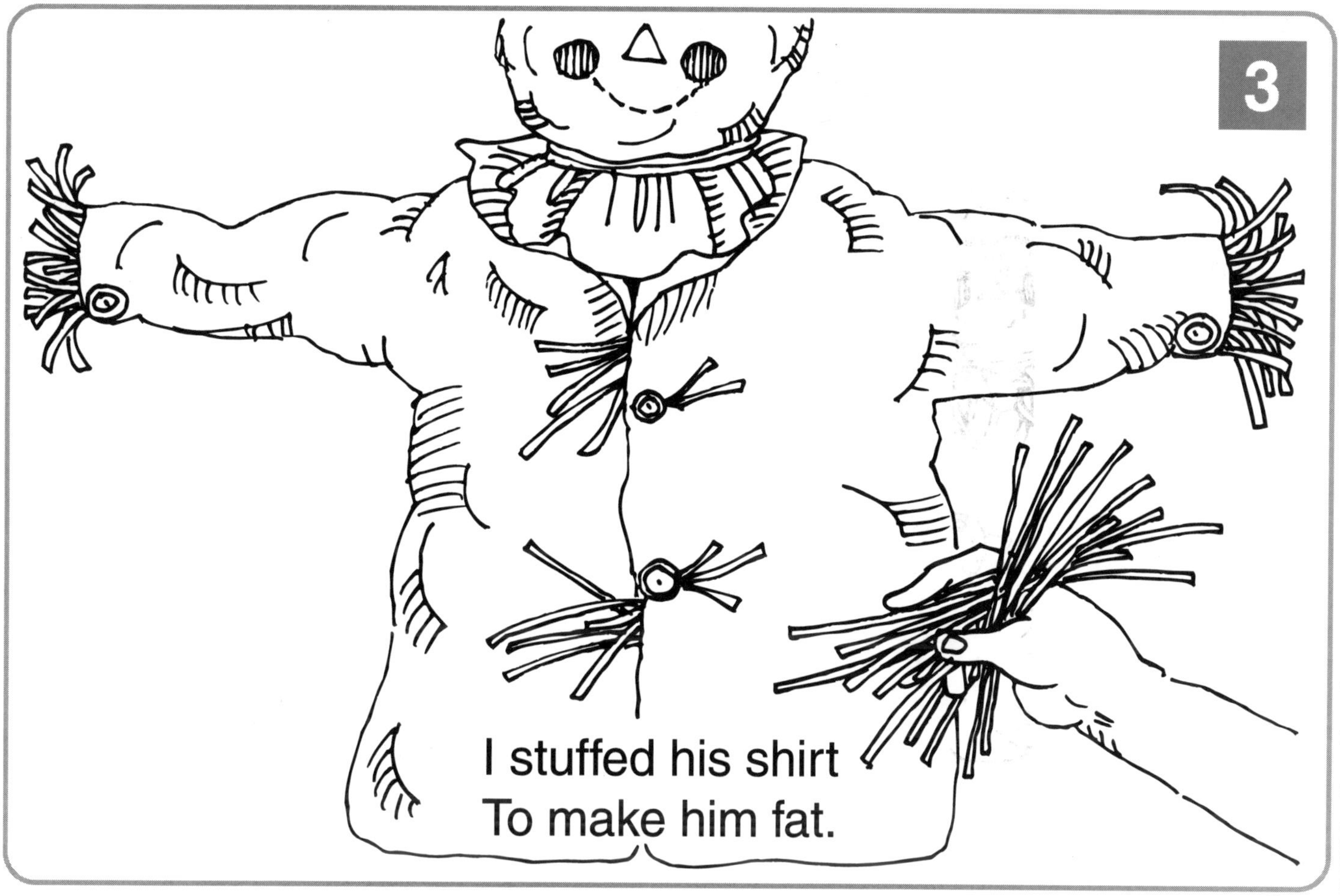

3

I stuffed his shirt
To make him fat.

4

I stuffed his pants
And stood him there
To welcome friends
From everywhere.

Name ______________________

What Did the Story Say?

Write the steps in order.

1. ______________________
2. ______________________
3. ______________________
4. ______________________
5. ______________________

Word Box

Stand it up.

Stuff the shirt.

Stuff the head.

Stuff the pants.

Put on the hat.

Show how Mr. Scarecrow looks. Show someone he welcomes.

Name ____________________

Lots of Stuff

The word **stuff** can have different meanings. Read the sentences. Look at the pictures. Answer the questions.

The bear is **stuffed**.

What kind of stuffed animals do you have?

____

____

The man is **stuffed.**

When did you feel stuffed?

____

____

Stuff your hands into the mittens.

What do your mittens look like?

____

____

See all the **stuff** in the desk.

What is in your desk?

____

____

Name ______________________

Welcome, Friends!

Start with **A** and connect the dots.

R

Name ______________________________

Rhyme Time

Color, cut, and paste to show pairs that rhyme.

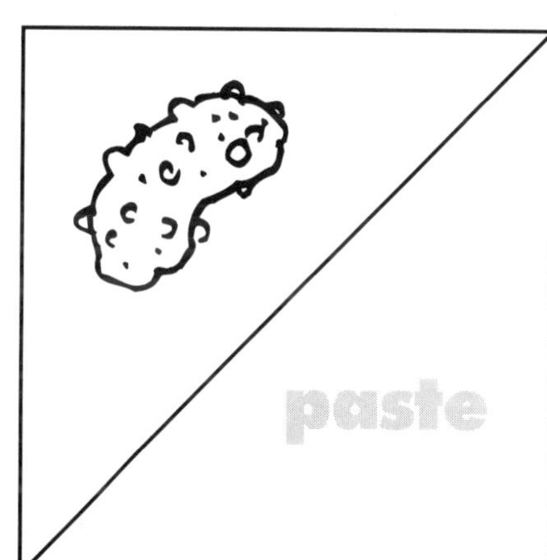

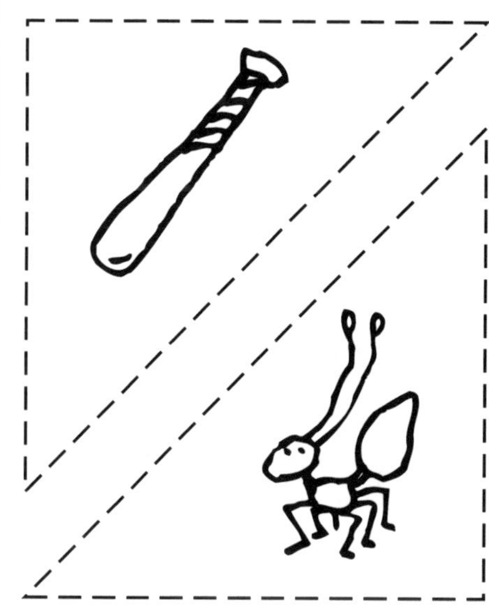

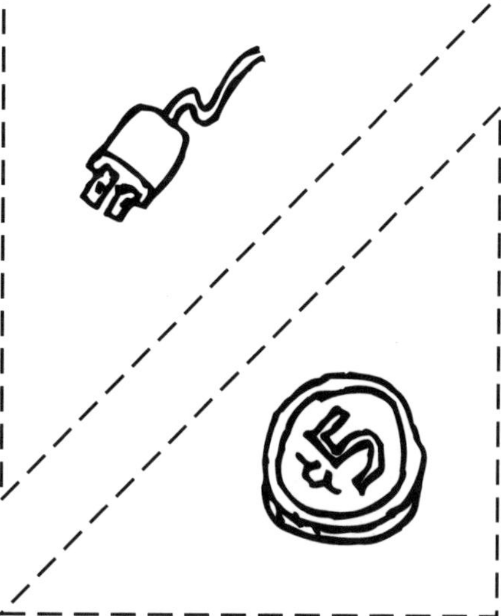

1

Heroes

Story Dictionary

sheriff

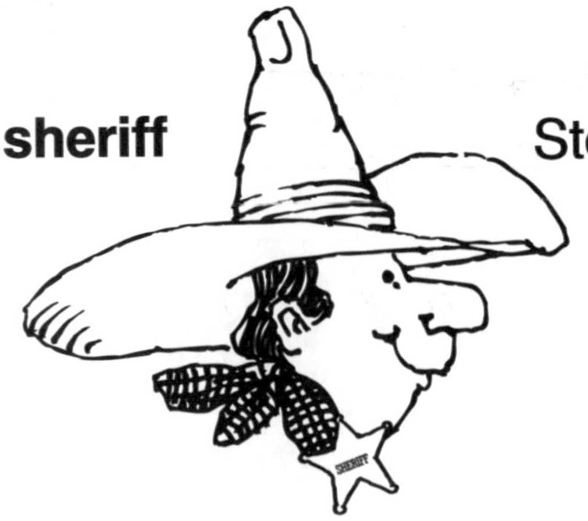
SHERIFF

knight

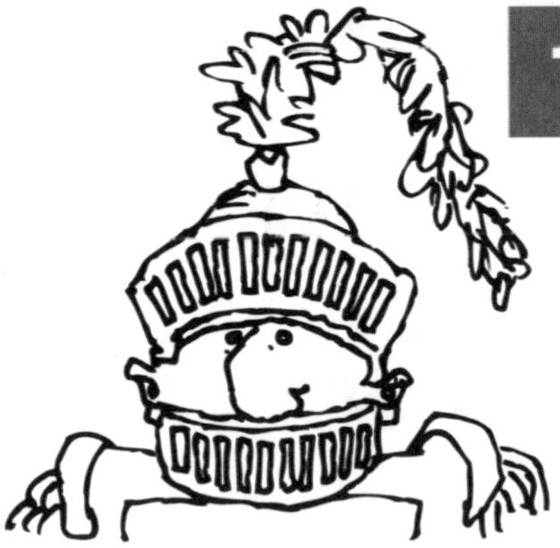

gold

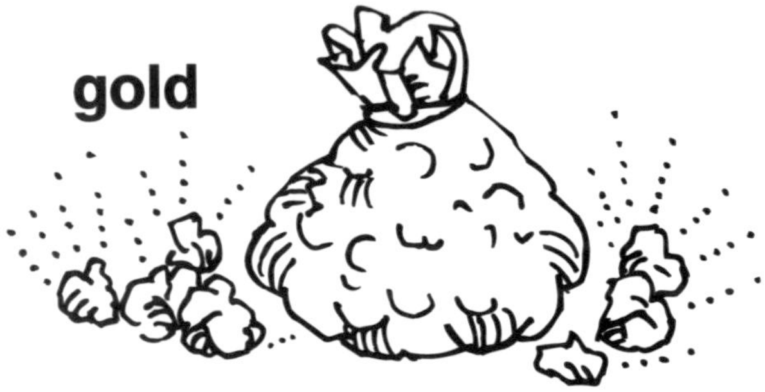

princess

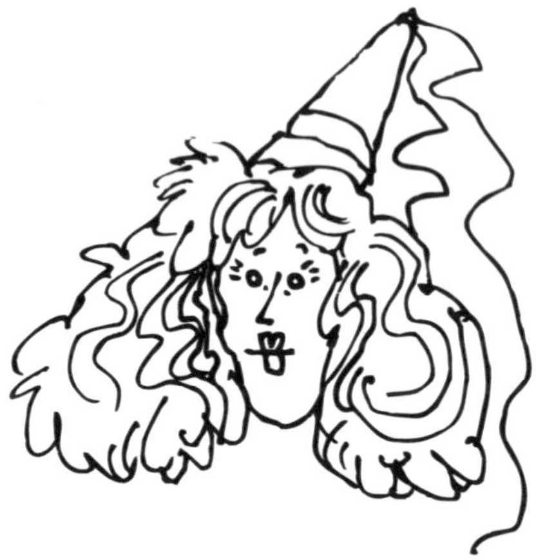

My book:

2

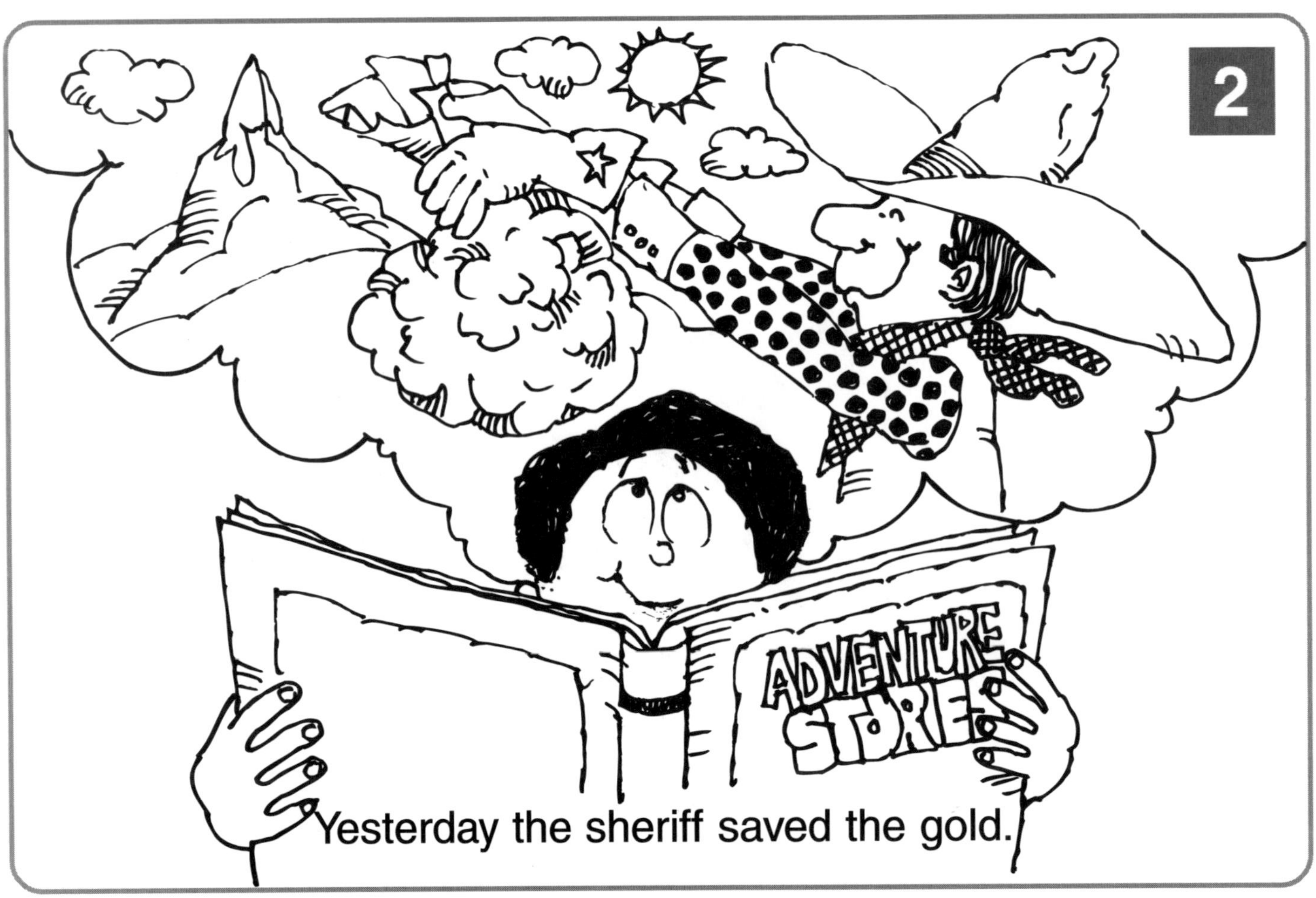
ADVENTURE
STORIES

Yesterday the sheriff saved the gold.

3

STORIES FOR YOU

Last night the knight saved the princess.

4

Books are filled with heroes who save the day.

Name ______________________________

What Did the Story Say?

Color, cut, and paste to show what the heroes did.

saved the

saved the

Think of a hero. Draw the hero and tell about what happened.

Name ______________________

Adding -*ed*

When **-ed** is added to some words, the silent e on the word is dropped first.

save + ed = saved

Add **-ed** to these words.
Remember to drop the silent e first.

save + ed = ___ ___ ___ ___ ___

tape + ed = ___ ___ ___ ___ ___

glue + ed = ___ ___ ___ ___ ___

skate + ed = ___ ___ ___ ___ ___ ___

slice + ed = ___ ___ ___ ___ ___ ___

sneeze + ed = ___ ___ ___ ___ ___ ___ ___

Write a sentence using one of the words you made.

____

____

____

Name ______________________________

Working with Word Families

-old

g + old = ___ ___ ___ ___   f + old = ___ ___ ___ ___

c + old = ___ ___ ___ ___   s + old = ___ ___ ___ ___

h + old = ___ ___ ___ ___   b + old = ___ ___ ___ ___

t + old = ___ ___ ___ ___   sc + old = ___ ___ ___ ___ ___

Write the words you made to complete the sentences.

The house will be __________.

He had a __________.

The necklace is __________.

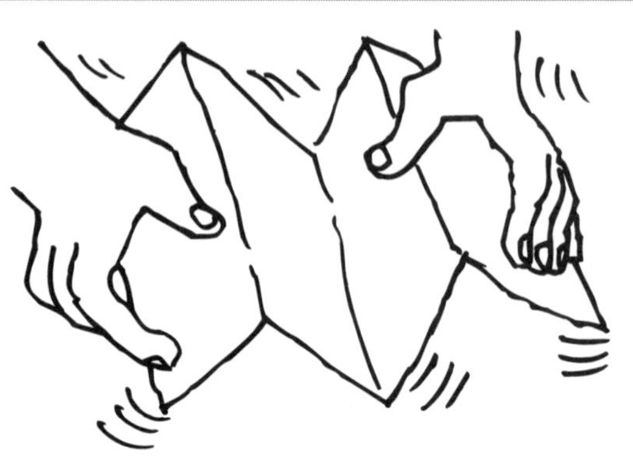

__________ the paper.

Name ______________________________

What's at the End?

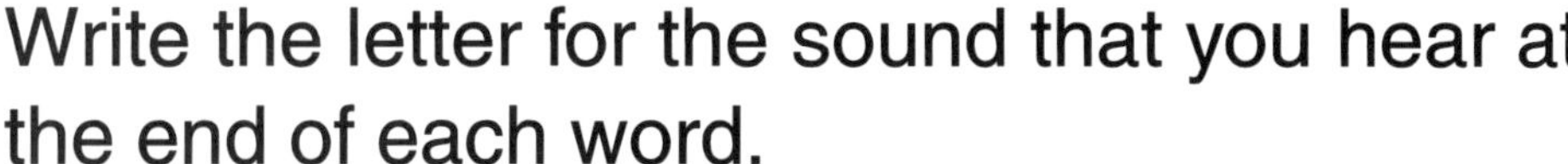

Write the letter for the sound that you hear at the end of each word.

What Do I See?

1

Story Dictionary

squirrels

sea

tree

sisters

dolphins

knee

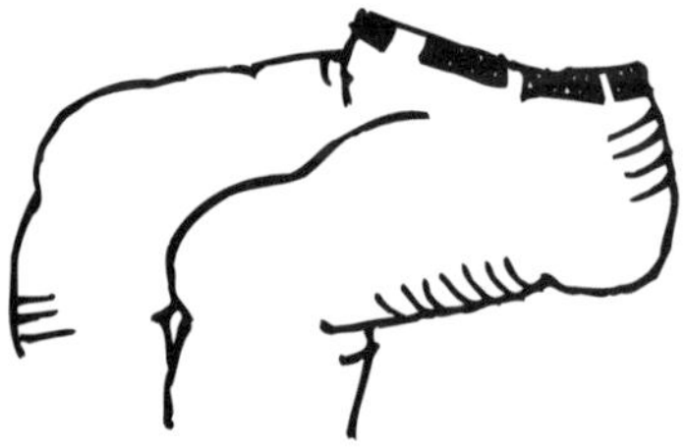

My book:

 70 EMC 745

2

Two little squirrels
Playing in the tree—
I see them and
They see me.

 70 EMC 745

3

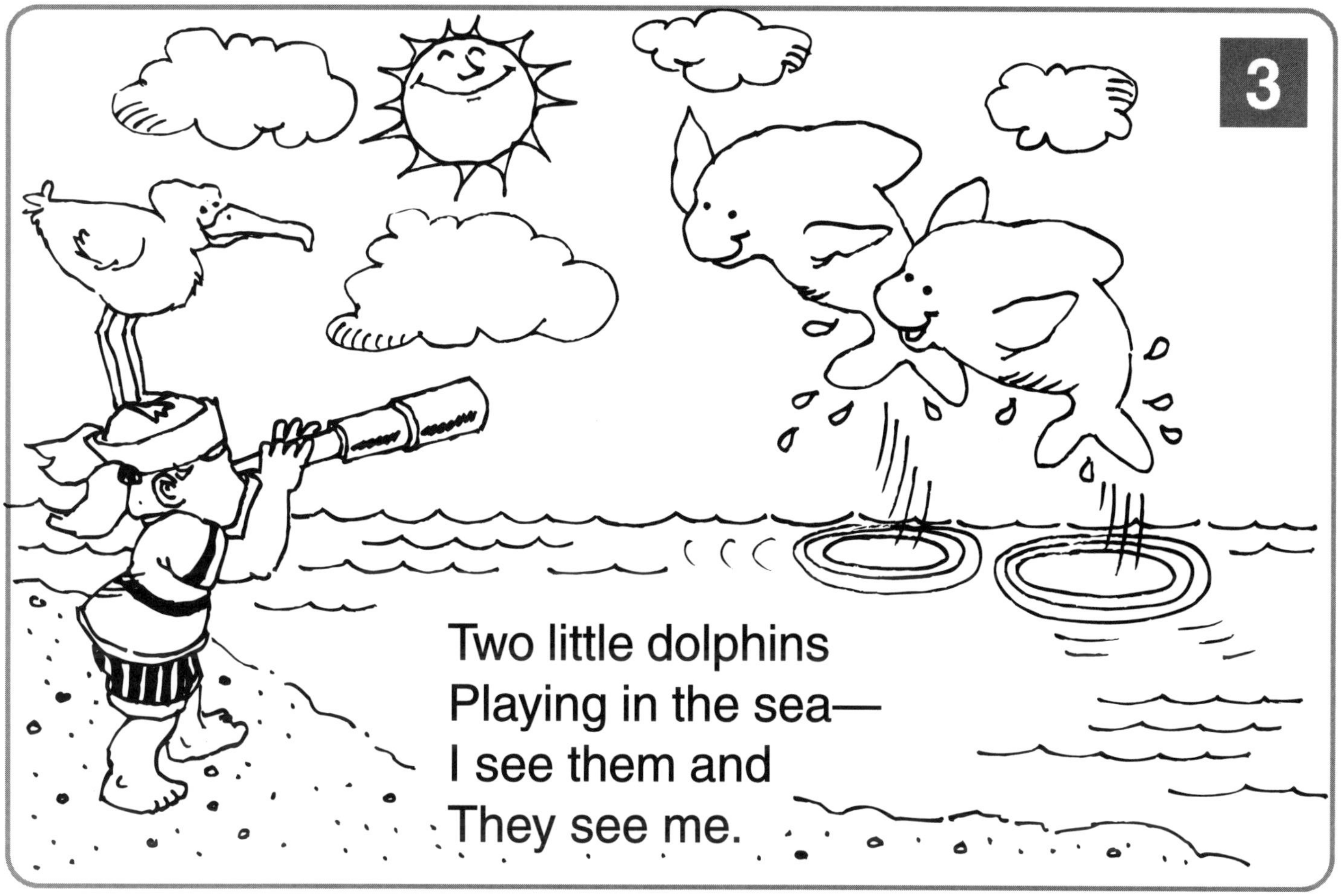

Two little dolphins
Playing in the sea—
I see them and
They see me.

4

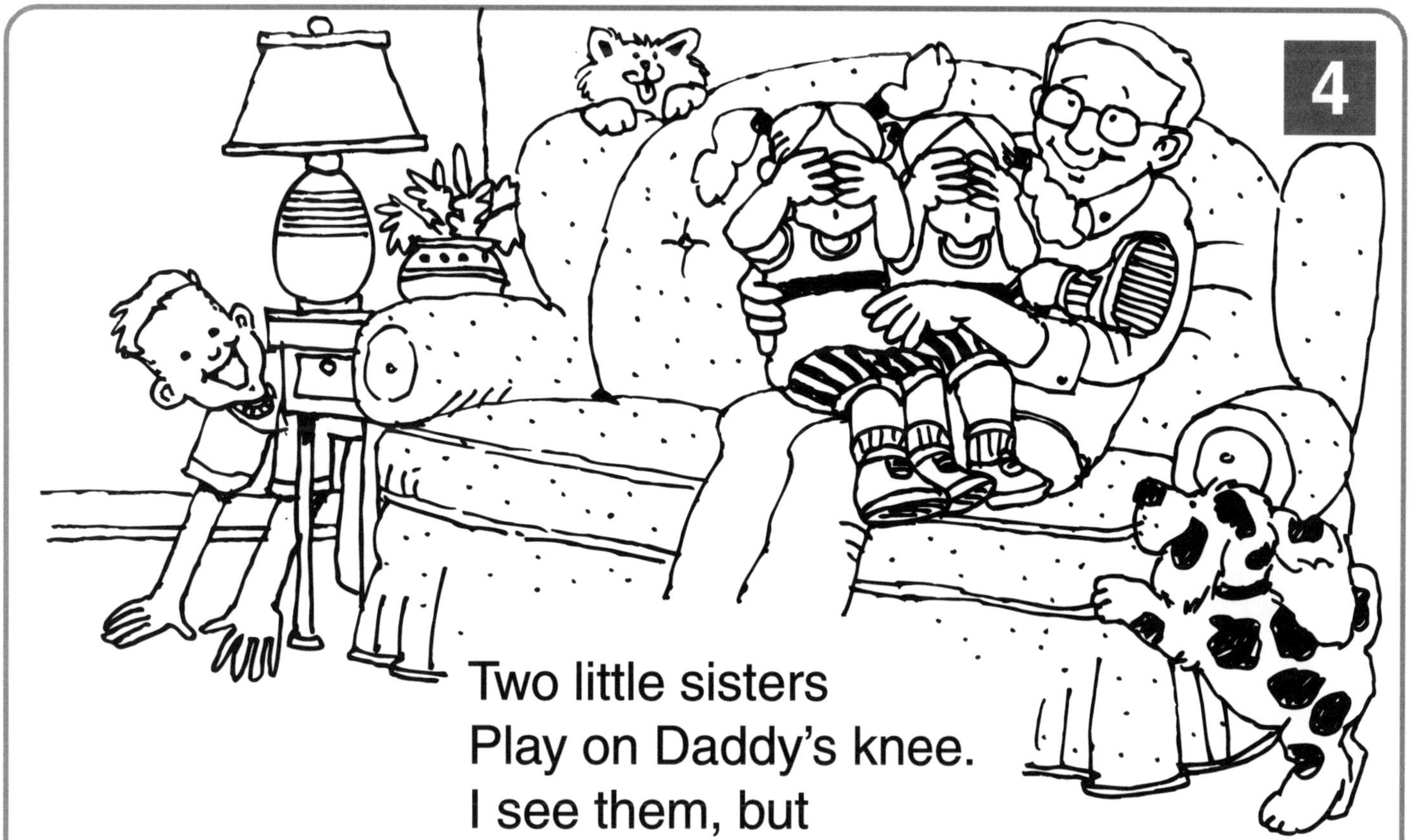

Two little sisters
Play on Daddy's knee.
I see them, but
They can't see me.

Name ____________________

What Did the Story Say?

Draw to show what was playing in the tree.	Draw to show what was playing in the sea.
Draw to show who was playing on Daddy's knee.	Think of a place that you like to play. Draw yourself playing there.

Name ______________________

More Than One

Write the word to tell how many. Add **s** to show more than one.

 ______	 ______
 ______	 ______
 ______	 ______
 ______	 ______

Word Box

squirrel sister dolphin tree

Name ______________________

What Do You See?

Look at the picture. Answer the questions.

Where's the starfish?

____

Where's the crab?

____

Where's the shell?

____

Where's the dolphin?

____

Word Box

in the shell	on the sand
on the rock	in the water

Name ___________________________

A Spyglass

Color, cut, and tape to make the spyglass.
Look through it and write about what you see on another paper.

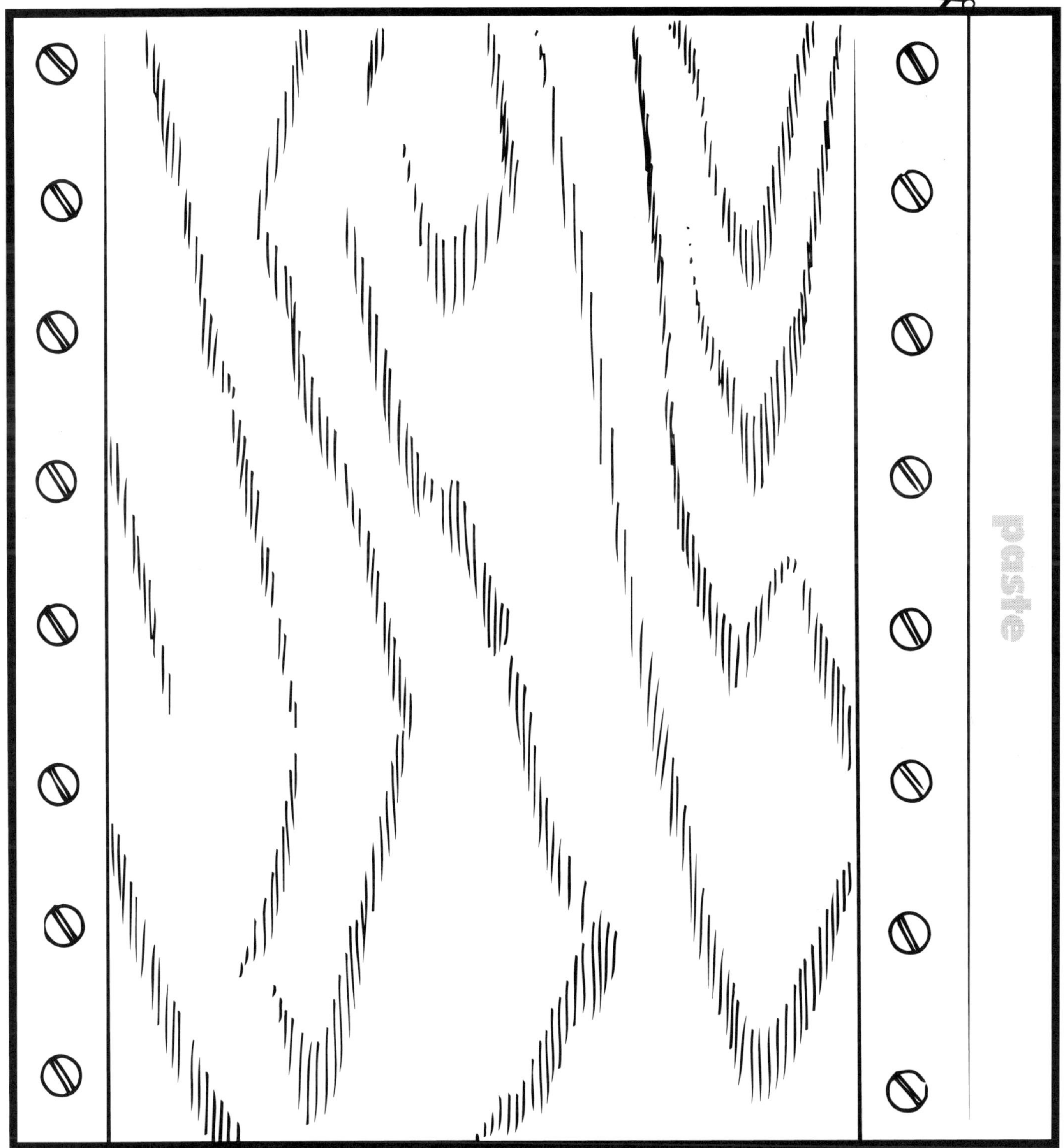

The Same and Not the Same

1

Story Dictionary

pick

carrots

snack

seeds

My book:

2

My great-grandpa planted seeds with my grandpa.

My grandpa planted seeds with my dad.

My dad plants seeds with me.

It is the same and not the same.

My great-grandpa picked carrots with my grandpa.

My grandpa picked carrots with my dad.

My dad picks carrots with me.

It is the same and not the same.

EMC 745

My great-grandpa eats a snack with my grandpa.
My grandpa eats a snack with my dad.
My dad eats a snack with me.

It is the same!

EMC 745
77

Name ______________________

What Did the Story Say?

Write three things that happened in the story.

1. ______________________

2. ______________________

3. ______________________

What different ways were the seeds planted?

____

____

What different ways were the carrots carried?

____

____

What was the same?

____

____

Name ______________________

Working with Word Families

-ame

fl + ame = ___ ___ ___ ___ ___ c + ame = ___ ___ ___ ___

fr + ame = ___ ___ ___ ___ ___ t + ame = ___ ___ ___ ___

g + ame = ___ ___ ___ ___ s + ame = ___ ___ ___ ___

Use the words you made to complete these sentences:

I put the photo in a ____________________.

Hide and Seek is my favorite ____________________.

My grandpa ____________________ to see me.

The ____________________ kitten licked my hand.

Write your own sentence using an **-ame** word.

____

Name ______________________________

Generations

Write the words in order to tell who is the oldest.

Word Box			
girl	grandpa	dad	great-grandpa

1. ____________________

2. ____________________

3. ____________________

4. ____________________

Write the two words that work together to make these compound words.

grandson ______________ + ______________

grandmother ______________ + ______________

grandfather ______________ + ______________

granddaughter ______________ + ______________

grandparent ______________ + ______________

grandchild ______________ + ______________

grandpa ______________ + ______________

grandma ______________ + ______________

Name ______________________________

Think and Draw

Show something you and your dad might do.

Did your dad do the same thing with your grandpa? Yes No
Tell how it was the same and how it was not the same.

____

____

Show something you and your mom might do.

Did your mom do the same thing with your grandma? Yes No
Tell how it was the same and how it was not the same.

____

____

The Hole That Matt Dug

1

Story Dictionary

hole 

dog 

ball 

boy 

My book:

2

This is the hole that Matt dug.
This is the ball that rolled into the hole that Matt dug.

3

This is the dog who saw the ball that rolled into the hole that Matt dug.

This is the boy who heard the dog that saw the ball that rolled into the hole that Matt dug.

4

This is Matt who dug the hole, rolled the ball, heard the bark, and found his ball.

Name ______________________________

What Did the Story Say?

Cut and paste to show the order.

First	Third
paste	paste
Second	**Fourth**
paste	paste

Write one sentence to tell what Matt did.

____

Name ______________________

Good Diggers

Color the pictures to show which things are good for digging. Draw a circle around the ones that you have used.

Name ______________________

Working with Word Families

-ug

Color, cut, and paste to show what each word means.

paste b + ug = ___ ___ ___	paste sl + ug = ___ ___ ___ ___	paste t + ug = ___ ___ ___
paste d + ug = ___ ___ ___	paste j + ug = ___ ___ ___	paste h + ug = ___ ___ ___

Write some other **-ug** words here.

____

____

Name ____________________

Big, Bigger, Biggest

Read all the boxes before you begin.

Draw a big hole.	Draw a bigger hole.
Draw the biggest hole.	Show what you would put in the hole.

Mr. Snowman

1

Story Dictionary

ball

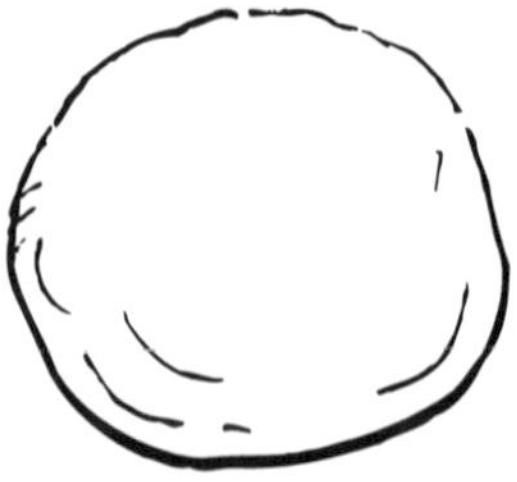

hat

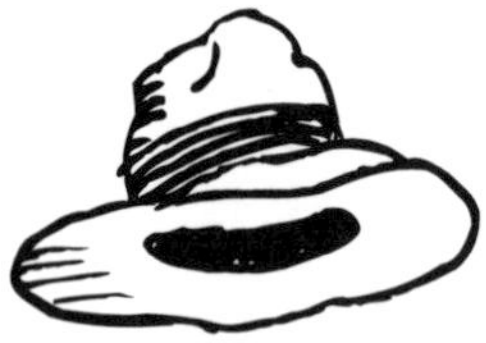

twig

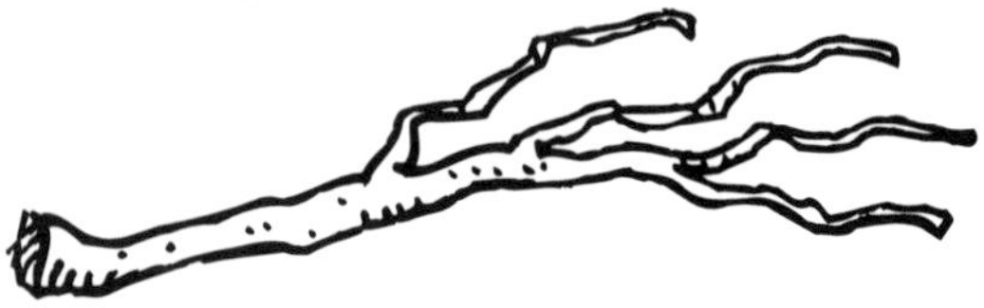

snowman

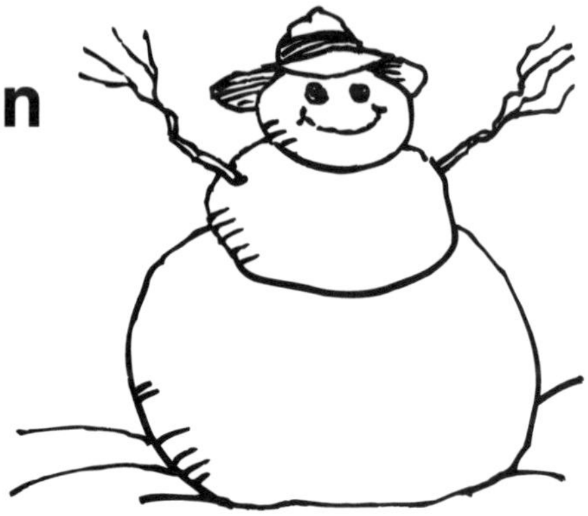

eyes

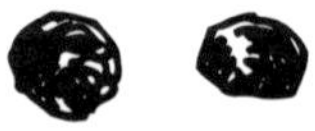

My book:

2

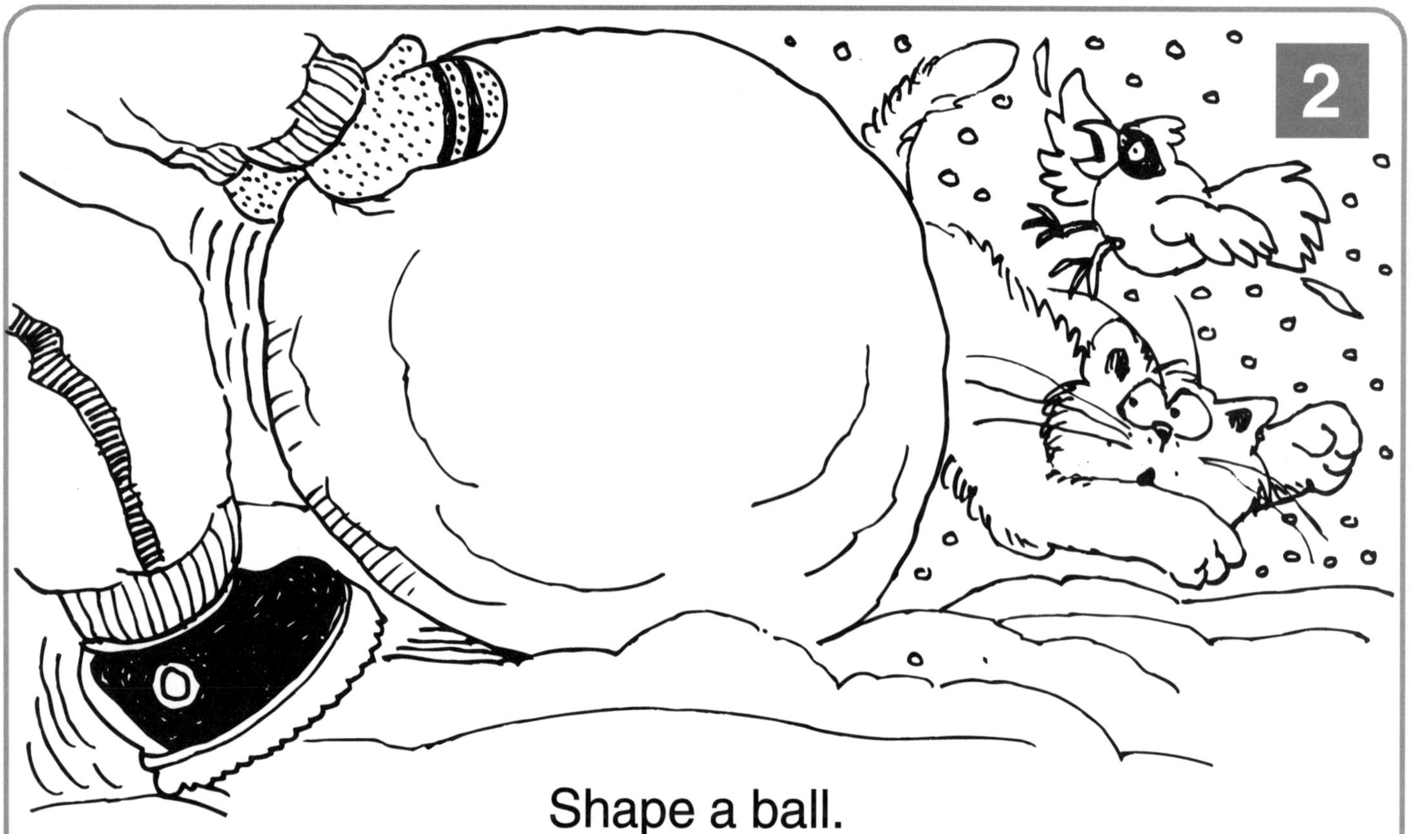

Shape a ball.
Roll it big.

88

3

Make another.
Add a twig.

4

Then one more,
Two eyes, a hat.
You made a snowman
Just like that!

EMC 745 89
©1999 by Evan-Moor Corp.

Name ______________________________

What Did the Story Say?

Put the steps in order.

1.	paste	2.	paste
3.	paste	4.	paste
5.	paste	6.	paste

Make another ball.	Add a twig.
Shape a ball.	Make another ball.
Add two eyes and a hat.	Roll it big.

Name ______________________

Snow Words

Write the two words that work together in these compound words. Color, cut, and paste to show what the words mean.

snowman	snowball
paste	paste
________ + ________	________ + ________
snowbank	snowflake
paste	paste
________ + ________	________ + ________
snowplow	snowshoe
paste	paste
________ + ________	________ + ________

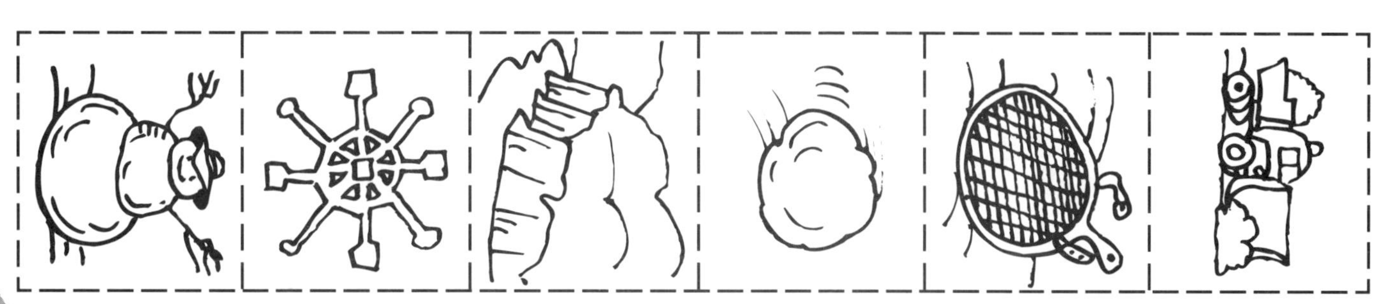

Name ______________________

Rhyming Words

Color the pictures that rhyme with **snow**.

 crow	 otter	 bow
 rocket	 sew	 throw

1. The cowboy said, “Whoa!” Does **whoa** rhyme with snow? Yes No

2. Mother said, “Yes!” Does **yes** rhyme with snow? Yes No

3. The sign said, “Slow.” Does **slow** rhyme with snow? Yes No

4. The light said, “Go.” Does **go** rhyme with snow? Yes No

Name ___________________________

On a Sunny Day

Color and cut out the pictures. Paste them in order.
Write about what happened on another paper.

1	2
3	4

I Can See the Moon

1

Story Dictionary

lights 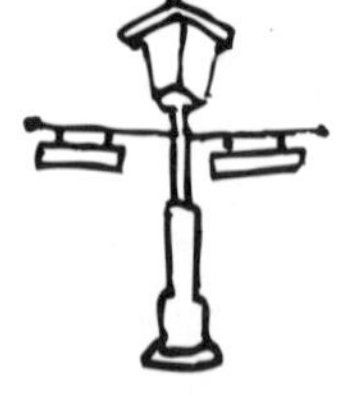

horn 

train 

moon 

horses 

chickens 

coop 

houses 

My book:

2

Lights flash on and off.
Horns honk and the train rumbles by.
It is nighttime at my house. I can see the moon.

3

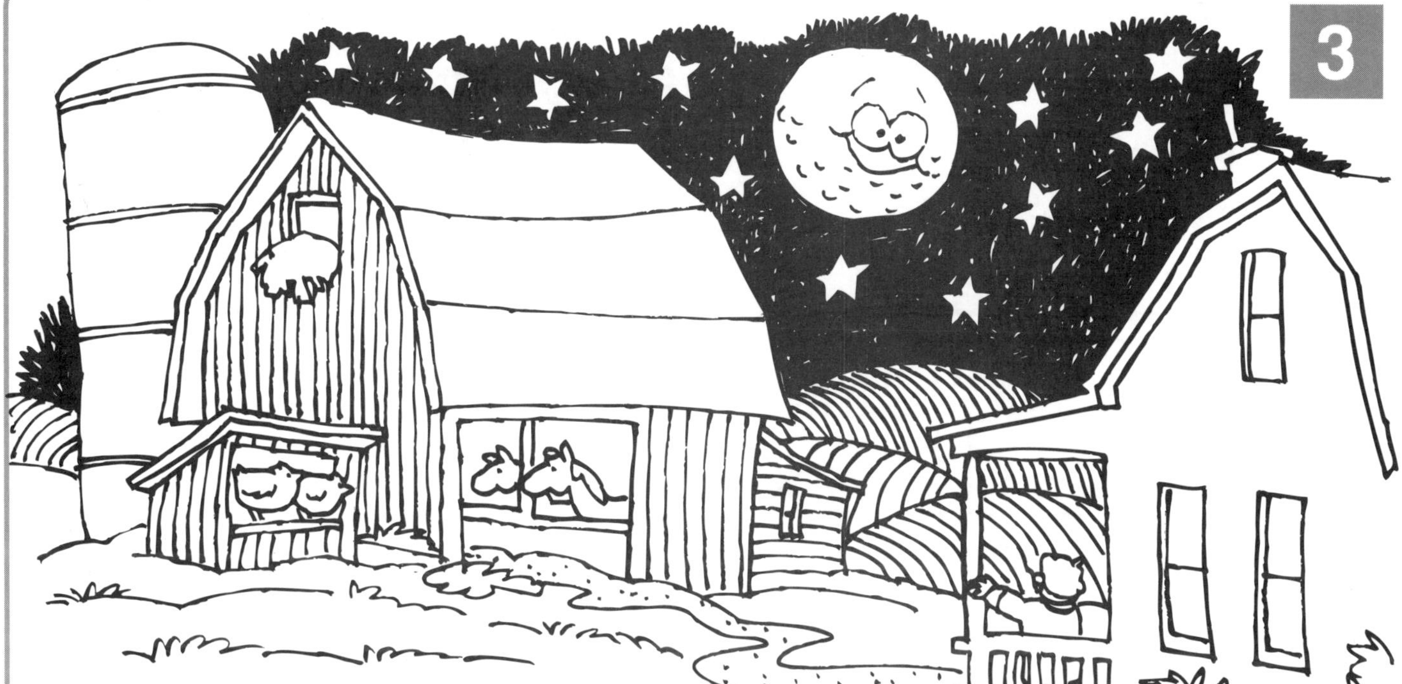

The horses whinny softly.
The chickens roost in the coop.
It is nighttime at my house. I can see the moon.

4

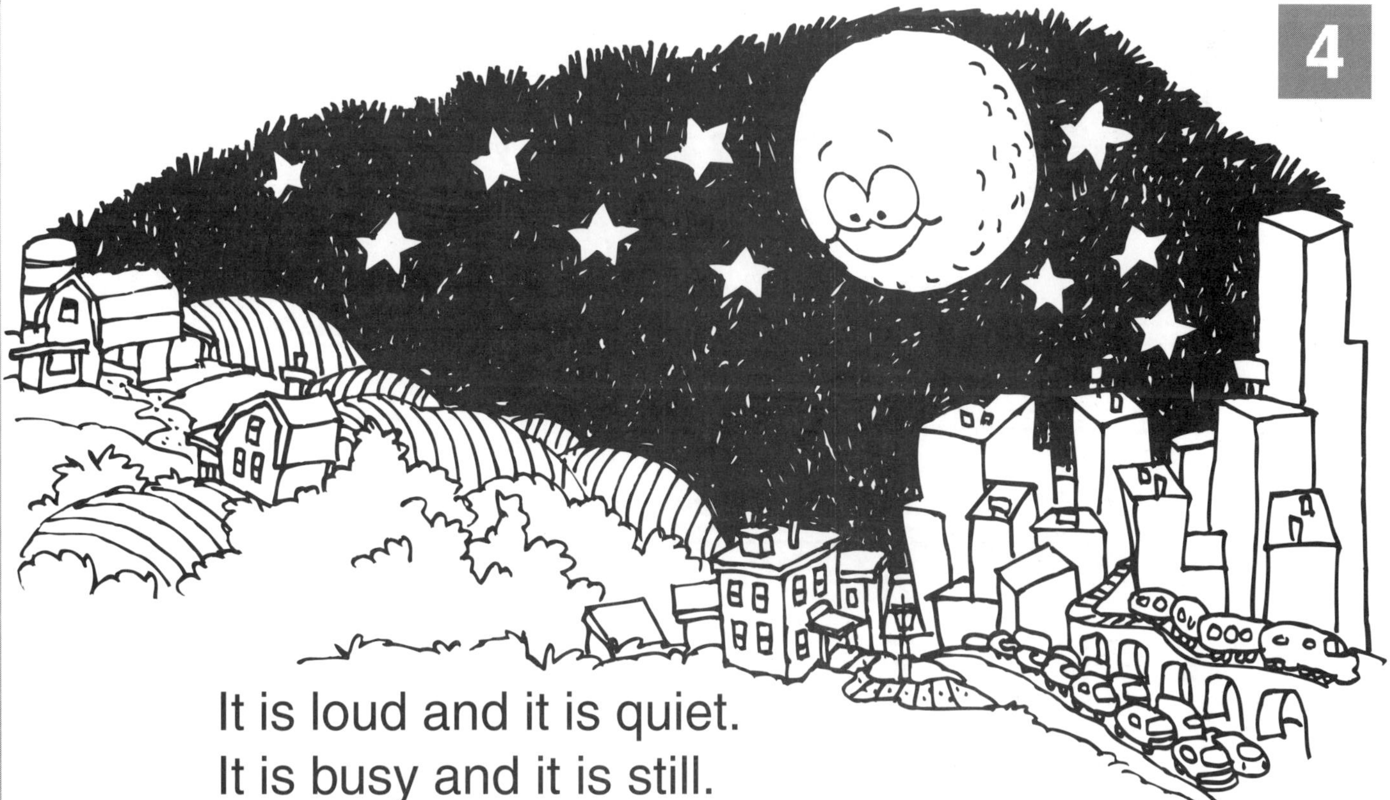

It is loud and it is quiet.
It is busy and it is still.
It is nighttime and the moon is in the sky.

Name ______________________

What Did the Story Say?

Cut and paste to tell what happened in the city and what happened in the country.

paste | paste

City

paste | paste

---

paste | paste

Country

paste

✂ -

Chickens roost.	Horns honk.	Lights flash.	Horses whinny.	Trains rumble.	The moon shines.	The moon shines.

Name ______________________

Opposites

Write a word to name each picture.
Draw a line to connect the opposites.

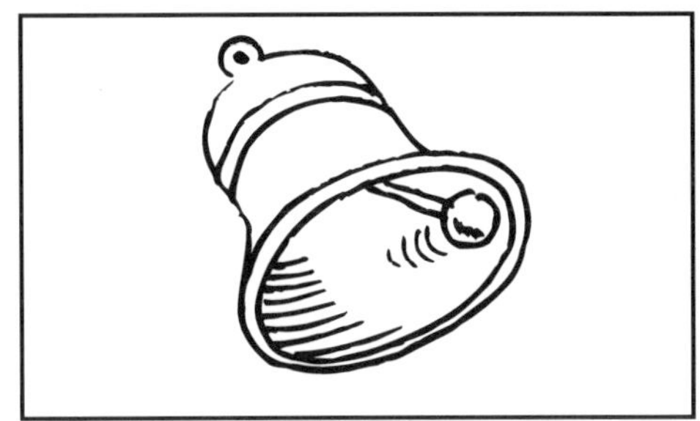

____

____

____

____

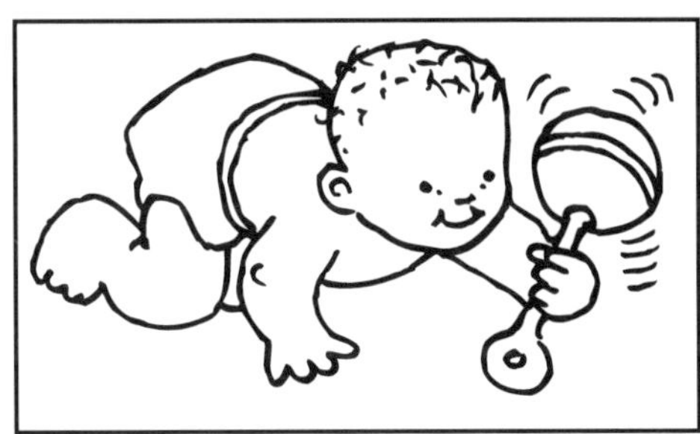

____

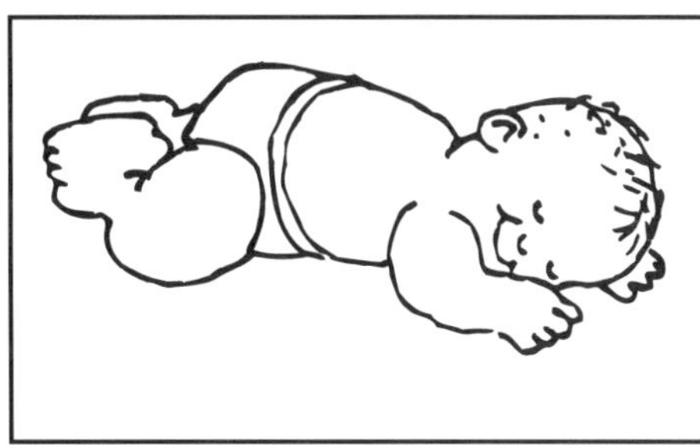

____

Word Box		
loud	quiet	busy
still	nighttime	daytime

Name ______________________________

City or Country?

Color, cut, and paste. Show which things you would find in the country and which things you would find in the city.

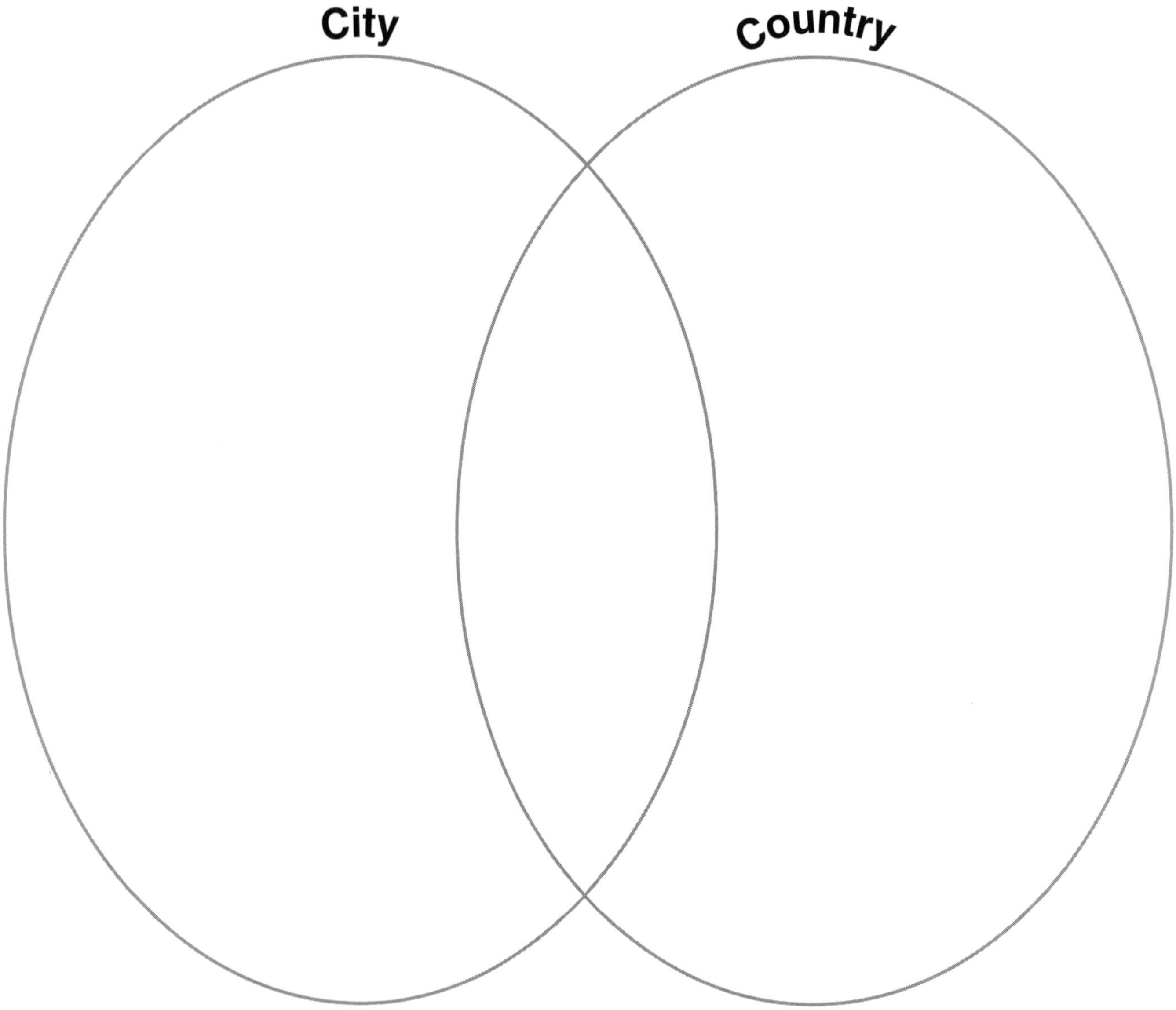

City

Country

Are there things that you might find in **both** the city and the country? Put them in the middle section.

Name ____________________________

Nighttime at My House

Draw a picture to show the things you see and hear when it is nighttime at your house. Then write to tell about your picture.

At the Amusement Park

1

Story Dictionary

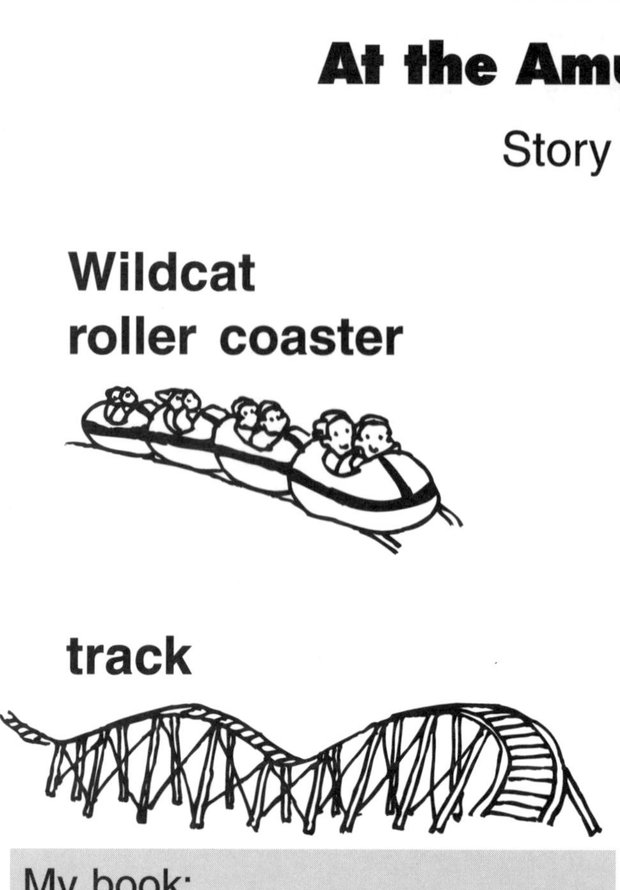

Wildcat roller coaster

track

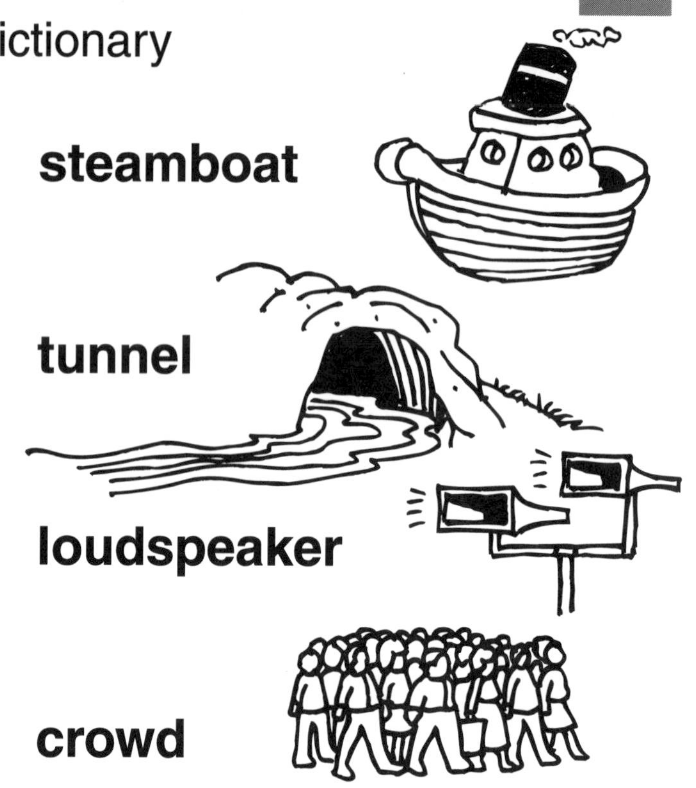

steamboat

tunnel

loudspeaker

crowd

My book:

EMC 745

2

The Wildcat zipped down the track.
Chelsea yelled, “Let’s go on the coaster. I can’t wait!”
Tori answered, “Not me, I don’t like roller coasters.”

3

The little steamboat chugged into the tunnel.
Chelsea yelled, “Look! Let’s ride on the boat. I can’t wait!”
Tori answered, “Not me, I don’t like dark tunnels.”

4

The loudspeaker boomed over the crowd, “The park is closing. Time to go home.”
Tori yelled, “Come on! Race you to the car!”
Chelsea answered, “Not me, I don’t want to leave.”

Name ______________________

What Did the Story Say?

Circle the correct name.

I like steamboats.	Chelsea	Tori
I don't like roller coasters.	Chelsea	Tori
I don't like going home.	Chelsea	Tori
I don't like dark tunnels.	Chelsea	Tori
I like amusement parks.	Chelsea	Tori

Write a sentence that tells what you know about each girl.

Chelsea: ______________________

____

Tori: ______________________

____

Name ______________________________

Compound Words

Cut and paste to make three compound words.
Draw a picture to show what each word means. Then write a sentence using each word.

paste	paste

paste	paste

paste	paste

wild	steam	loud
boat	speaker	cat

Name ______________________

A Contraction Crossword

1.	'	2.		3.

Across

1. ________ like to go on the roller coaster.
4. I ____________ go today.
5. It ______________ too scary.

Down

2. I ____________ like dark tunnels.
3. ________________ hurry!

Word Box		
isn't	Let's	can't
don't	I'd	

Name ___________________________

Working with Word Families

-ace

gr + ace = ___ ___ ___ ___ ___

r + ace = ___ ___ ___ ___

sp + ace = ___ ___ ___ ___ ___

l + ace = ___ ___ ___ ___

pl + ace = ___ ___ ___ ___ ___

f + ace = ___ ___ ___ ___

Use one of the words you made to make a compound word that names the pictures.

+ ______________ =

fire______________

+ ______________ =

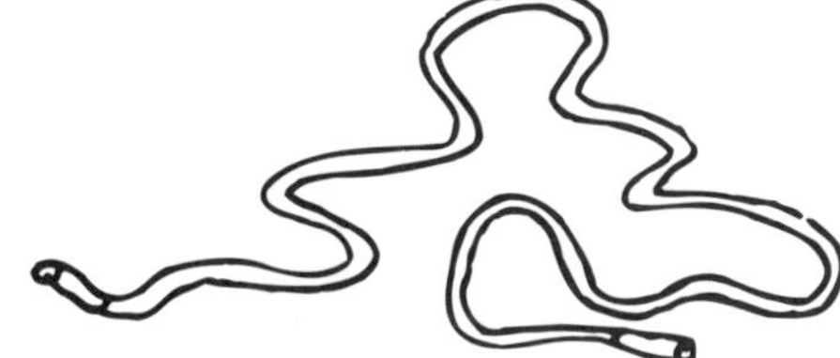

shoe______________

Traveling

1

Story Dictionary

store

jet plane

bus

clouds

train

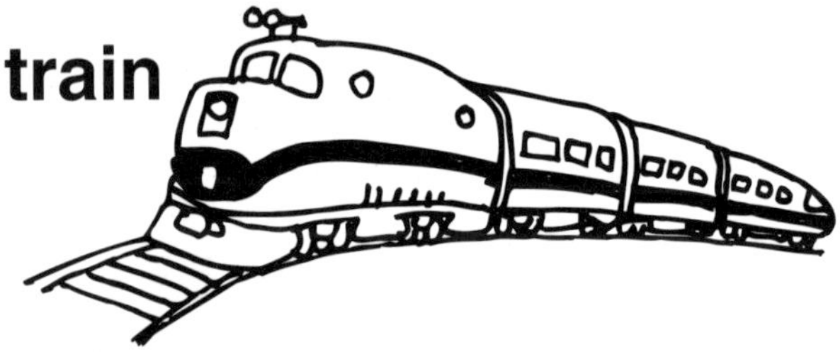

back seat

My book:

2

Going to the store,
Biking down the street,
Going to Grandma's in Mom's back seat,

3

Riding on a bus,
Sleeping on a train,
Flying through the clouds in a big jet plane—

4

I'm traveling!

EMC 745 107 ©1999 by Evan-Moor Corp.

Name ____________________

What Did the Story Say?

List five ways to travel.

1. ____________________

2. ____________________

3. ____________________

4. ____________________

5. ____________________

Tell two places that the storyteller was going.

1. ____________________

2. ____________________

How do you like to travel?

____

Where do you like to go?

____

Name ______________________________

The Sound of *a*

Color the pictures whose names have the same vowel sound as **day**.

Name ______________________________

Traveling on Wheels

Draw a line to show which wheels you would use.

I take the baby for a walk.

I fly to Grandma's.

I pedal to the playground.

I pay the driver and sit down.

I sit in the back seat. When Mom stops, I hop out my door.

I move the big pumpkin from the garden to the porch.

Name ______________________________

A Fun Way to Travel

Connect the dots to see a fun way to travel. Start at **a**.

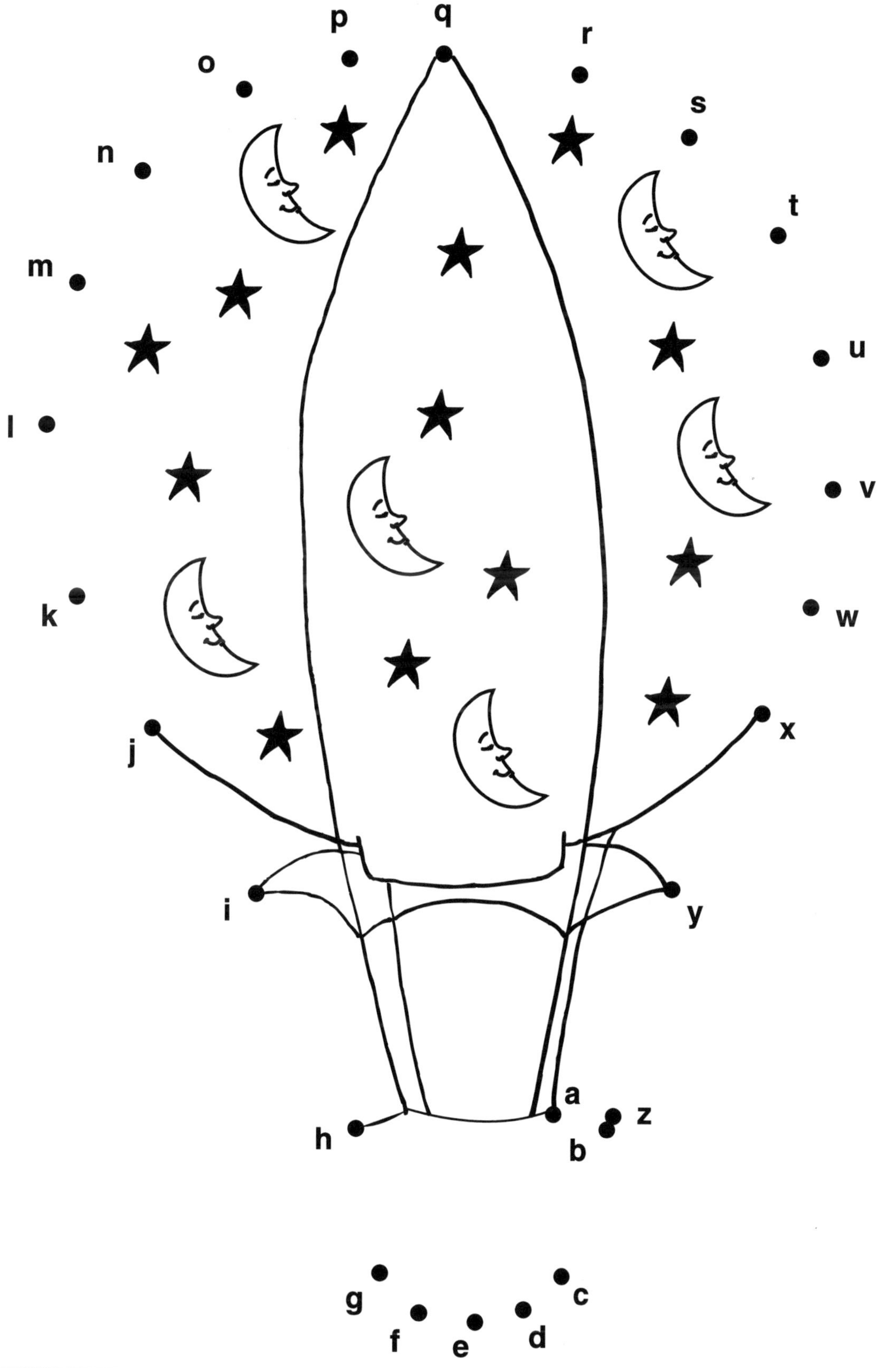

p q r o s n t m u l v k w j x i y a z h b g c f e d

senses

The Candy Store

1

Story Dictionary

gum balls

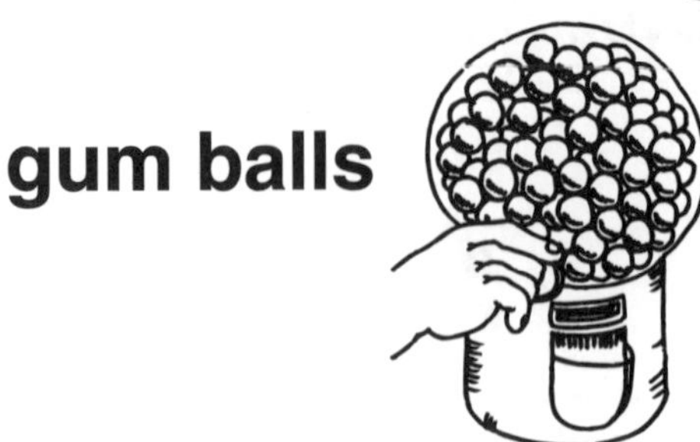

cookies

peppermint stick candy

penny

My book:

EMC 745

2

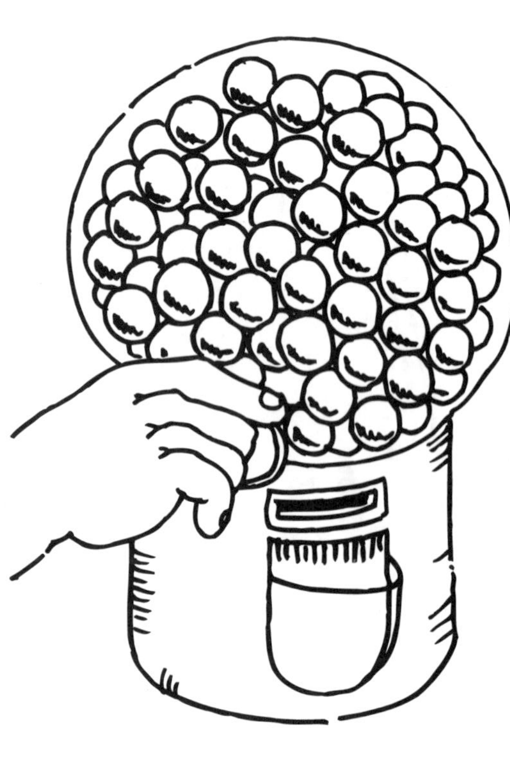

Gum balls for a penny.
I want three.
Peppermint stick candy
Buy it for me.

EMC 745

3

Cookies of chocolate
And sugar, too—
My stomach is growling
How about you?

4

I can taste with my nose
And smell with my eyes.
My mouth is all ready
For a sweet surprise.

Name ______________________

What Did the Story Say?

Write the three things you could buy at the candy store.

1. ______________________

2. ______________________

3. ______________________

Does the storyteller want to buy something? Yes No
Explain why you think so.

____

____

____

____

____

What would you buy at a candy store?

____

____

Name ____________________

Sweet and Sour

Write **sweet** or **sour** to tell how it would taste.

 ____________	 ____________
 ____________	 ____________
 ____________	 ____________

Draw something sweet that you like to eat.	Draw something sour that you like to eat.

Name ______________________________

The Sound of *sw*

Color the pictures whose names begin with the sound **sw** stands for.

How many did you find? ________

Name ______________________________

Using My Senses

Draw a line to show which sense you use.

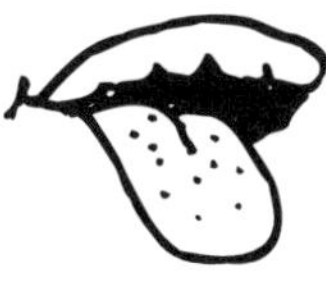

to feel

to see

to taste

to smell

to hear

Sometimes senses work together. Make an **X** to show which senses you would use.

	taste	smell	see	hear	feel
rose					
book					
ice cream cone					
cat					
fire truck					

1

Things to Do

Story Dictionary

seed

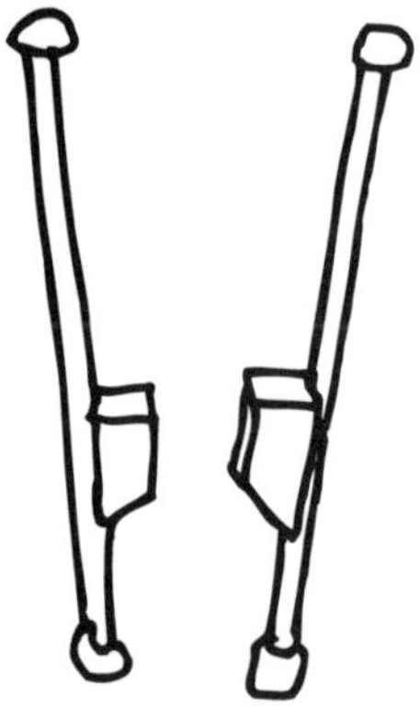

kite

ball

stilts

bike

stones

My book:

2

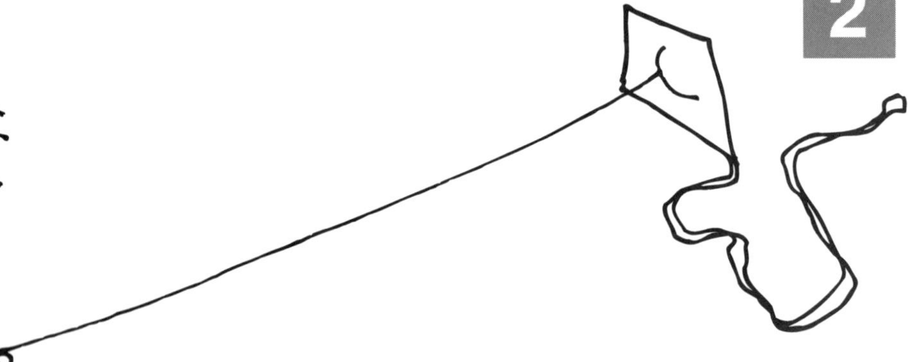

Plant a seed.
Fly a kite.
Kick a ball out of sight.

EMC 745 118 ©1999 by Evan-Moor Corp.

3

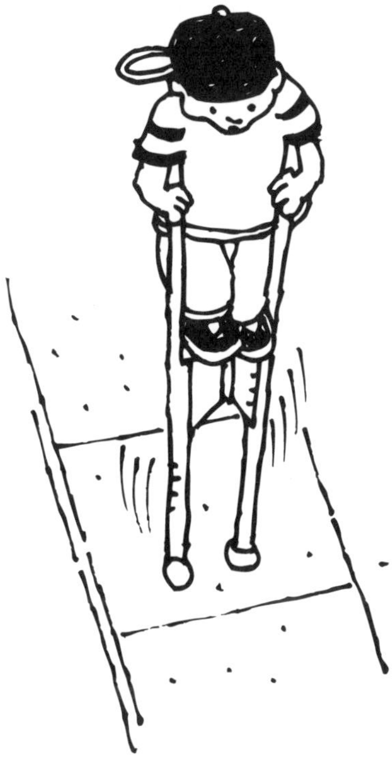

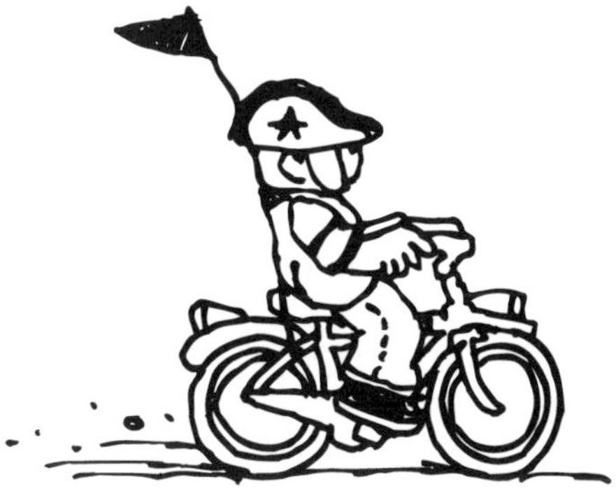

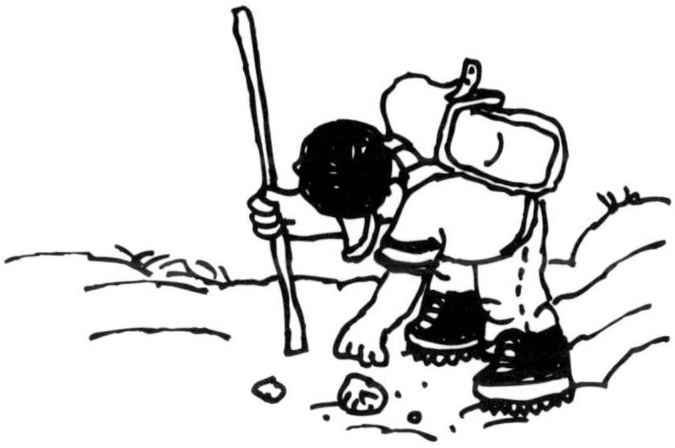

Walk on stilts.
Ride a bike.
Pick up stones as I hike.

4

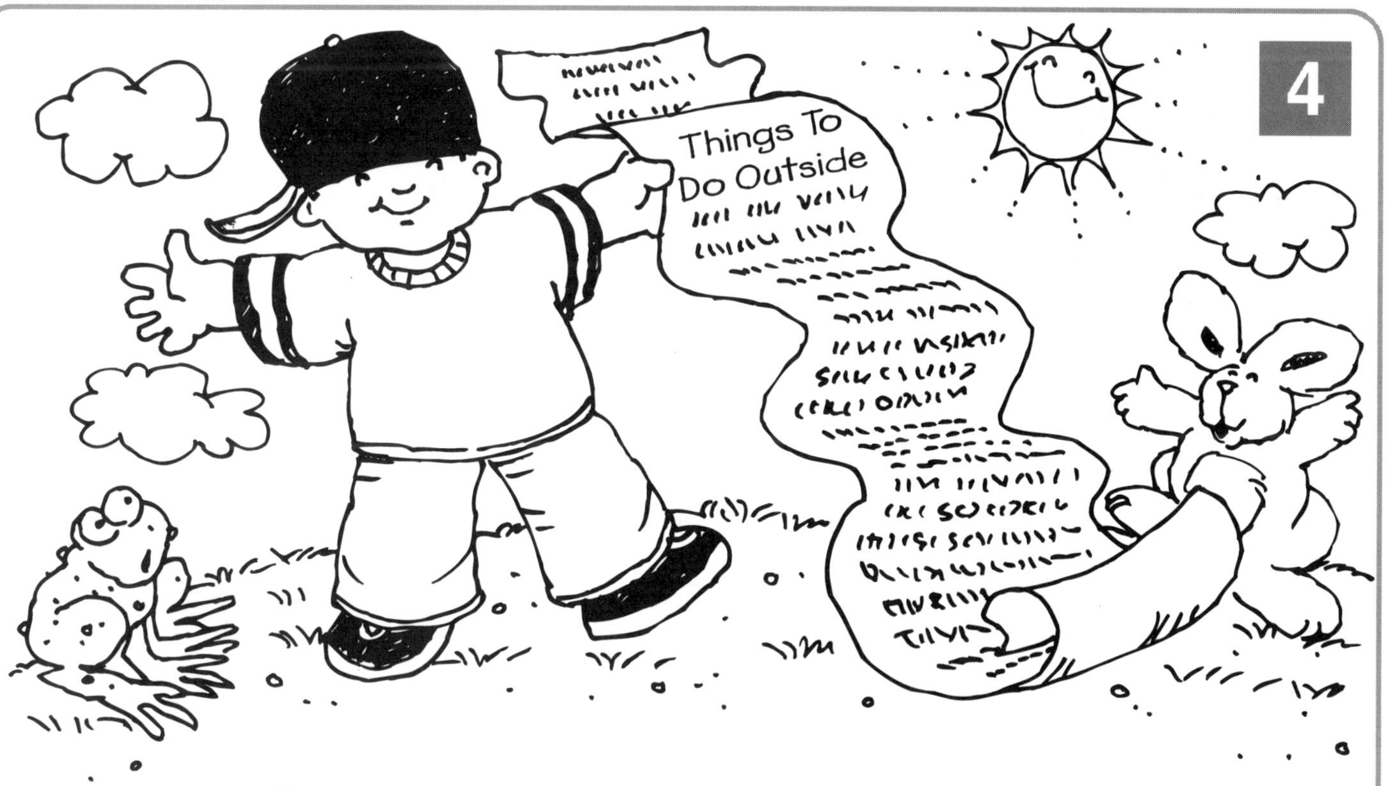

Come outside and play with me.
It's an adventure—don't you agree?

Name ______________________________

What Did the Story Say?

Color, cut, and paste to show the six things the storyteller did.

paste	paste	paste
paste	paste	paste

Name ______________________________

The Sound of *i*

Color the pictures whose names have the same vowel sound as **hike**.

Name ______________________________

An Adventure

Color and cut out the pictures. On another paper, paste them in order to tell the story of the adventure.

Name ______________________________

My List

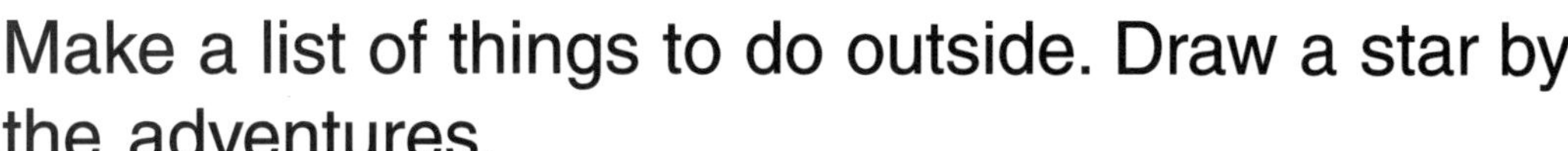

Make a list of things to do outside. Draw a star by the adventures.

1.

2.

3.

4.

5.

6.

Simple Machines

1

Story Dictionary

pulley

wheel

lever

screw

wedge

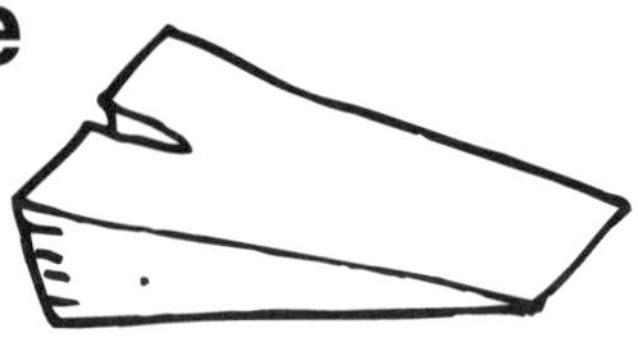

inclined plane

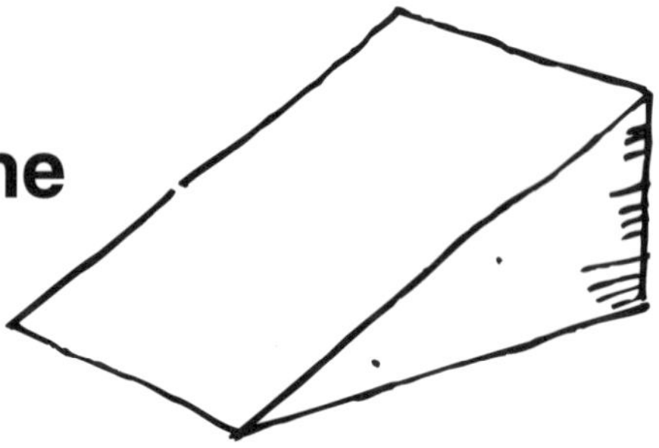

My book:

 124 EMC 745

2

There are six simple machines that help us do work.

 124 EMC 745

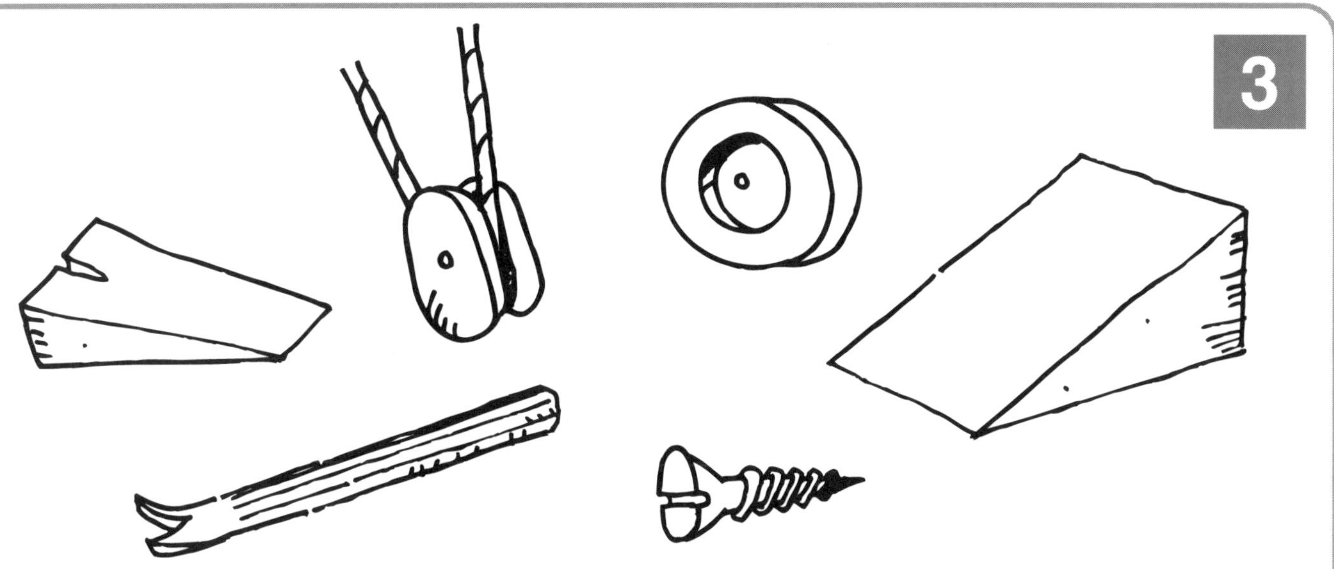

A pulley and a lever help lift heavy things.
A wedge helps cut things apart.
A screw holds things together.
A wheel makes moving easy.
An inclined plane is just a ramp.

Look all around you and find the simple machines that you use every day.

Name ______________________________

What Did the Story Say?

Cut and paste to make sentences. Paste the words to make a sentence.

	paste	is an inclined plane.
	paste	holds things together.
	paste	makes lifting a lid easy.
	paste	help us do work.
	paste	can lift something heavy.
	paste	makes moving easy.

A lever	A screw	Simple machines	A pulley	A wheel	A ramp

Name ____________________

Working with Word Families

-amp

Circle the word part that is the same.

scamp

clamp

lamp

ramp

stamp

Put each word from the box in the puzzle.

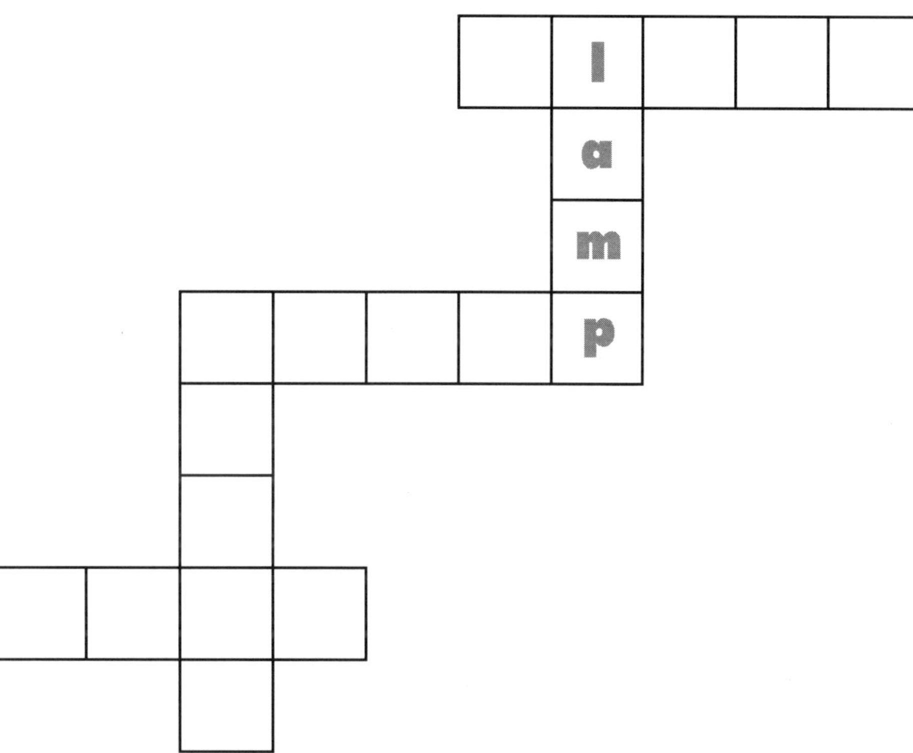

Use a word from the word box to complete each sentence.

I used the ______________ to hold the wood still.

I put a ______________ on the letter.

I pushed the cart up the ______________.

Will you please turn on the ______________?

Name ____________________

Using My Tools

Put the steps in order. Write about the steps on another paper.

1	2
3	4

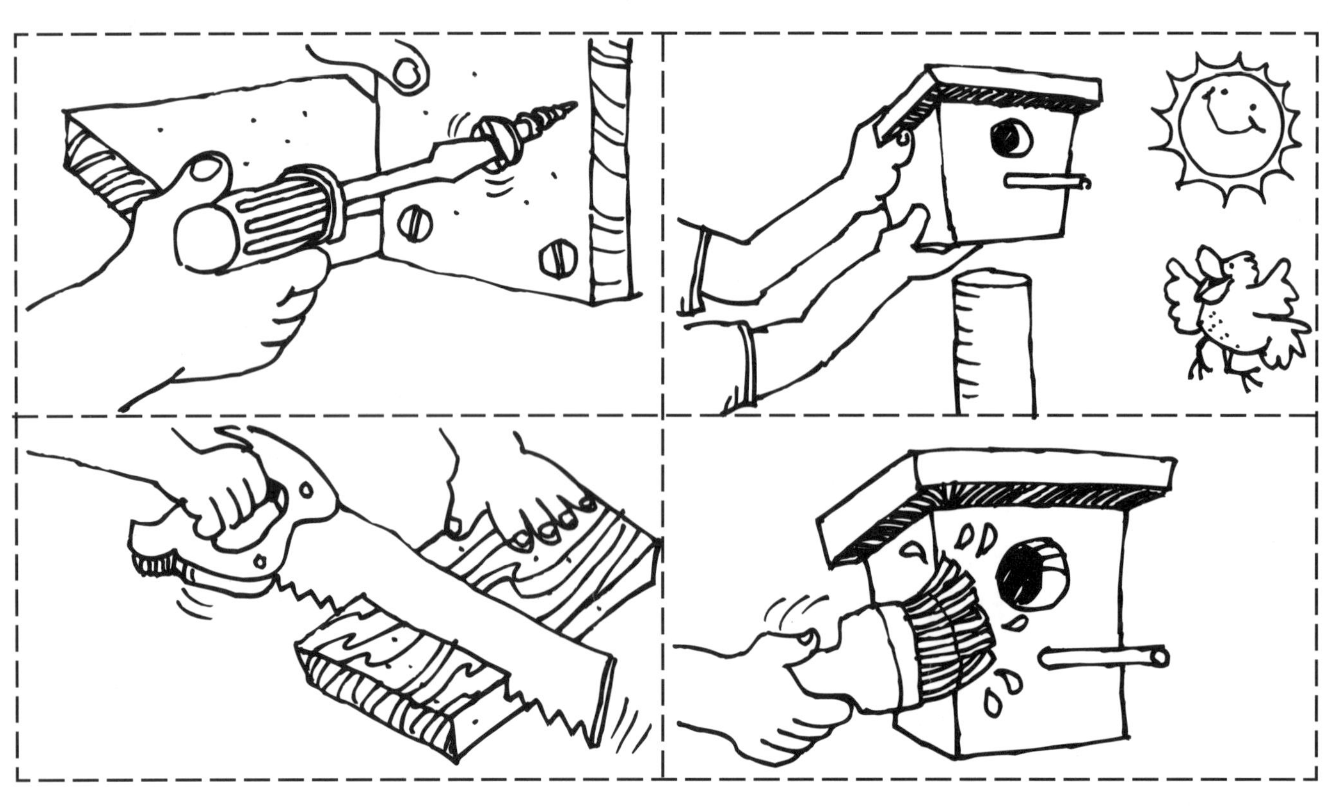

Name ____________________

Simple Machines at Work

Match the simple machine to the machine that is working.

paste	paste	paste
lever	inclined plane	pulley
paste	paste	paste
screw	wheel	wedge

Recycling

Story Dictionary

1

recycling

throw away

trash

My book:

2

Turning something old into something new is good.

Recycling is making something new from things that have been used.

We recycle when we make trash into something usable instead of throwing it away.

 131 EMC 745

Recycling means using the same things over and over. That takes less energy than making something new.

 131 EMC 745

Name ______________________

What Did the Story Say?

What is recycling?

____

____

Why is recycling good?

____

____

____

Do you recycle? Yes No

Tell what you do.

____

____

____

____

Name ____________________

Working with Word Families

-ash

cr + ash = ___ ___ ___ ___ ___

c + ash = ___ ___ ___ ___

fl + ash = ___ ___ ___ ___ ___

r + ash = ___ ___ ___ ___

sm + ash = ___ ___ ___ ___ ___

d + ash = ___ ___ ___ ___

sp + lash = ___ ___ ___ ___ ___ ___

tr + ash = ___ ___ ___ ___ ___

Use the words you made to complete the sentences.

The truck's lights ____________________ on and off.

I have to ____________________ or I will be late.

Please empty the ____________________.

Don't ____________________ water on the floor.

Name ______________________________

Using Things Again

Write a sentence to tell how you could reuse each thing.

Name ______________________

Remember to Recycle

Draw, color, and cut out the bookmarks. Use them over and over.

Using trash is good.

Saving energy is good.

Write your own recycling idea here.

The Hippopotamus

1

Story Dictionary

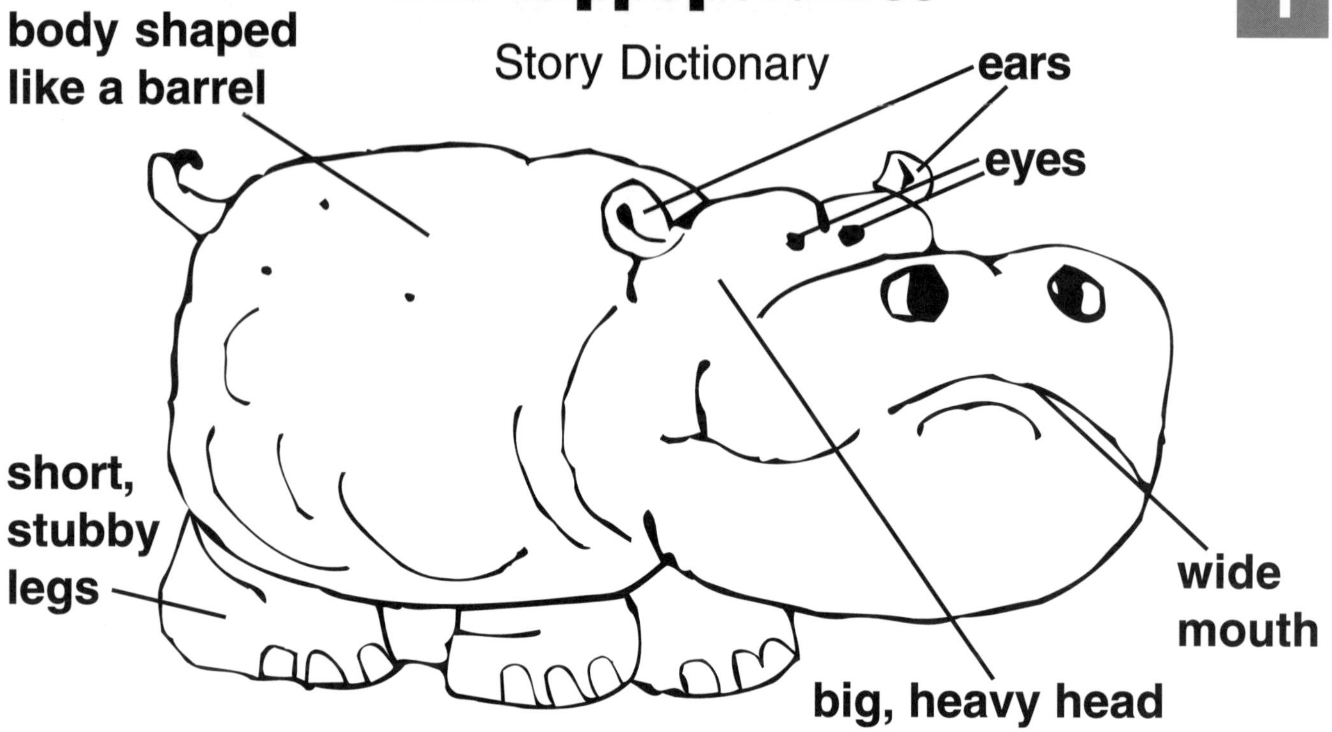

body shaped like a barrel

ears

eyes

short, stubby legs

wide mouth

big, heavy head

My book:

2

The hippopotamus lives near rivers and lakes in Africa. It spends its days in the water resting. It spends its nights on land looking for grass to eat.

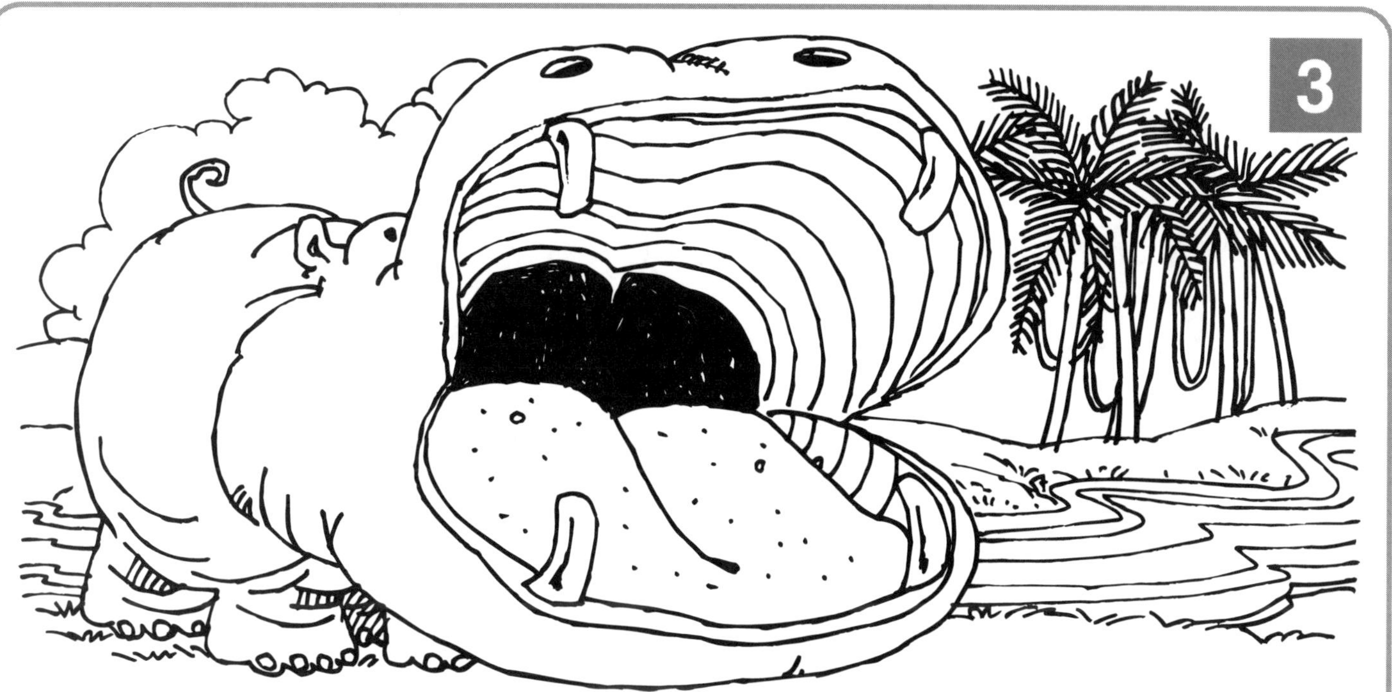

The hippo has short, stubby legs. Its body is shaped like a barrel. Its head is big and heavy. It can open its mouth wide.

Often when the hippo's body is underwater, its eyes and ears stick out. Sometimes the hippo goes all the way underwater and rests on the bottom. It can stay underwater for six minutes.

Name ______________________

What Did the Story Say?

Fill in the circle by the best answer.

Where do hippos live?

- ◯ They live in the desert.
- ◯ They live near rivers and lakes.
- ◯ They live in South America.

What do hippos do during the day?

- ◯ They look for grass to eat.
- ◯ They take a walk with a friend.
- ◯ They rest in the water.

What do hippos do at night?

- ◯ They swim in the water.
- ◯ They look for grass to eat.
- ◯ They wiggle their ears.

What is special about the hippo's eyes and ears?

- ◯ They are really big and floppy.
- ◯ They stick out when most of the hippo's body is underwater.
- ◯ They can open wide.

Write two things that you learned about hippos.

1. ______________________________

2. ______________________________

Name ______________________

The Sound of *o* at the End

Color the pictures whose names have the same ending sound as **hippo**.

Name ____________________

A Hippo Crossword Puzzle

							1.				
	2.										
3.								4.			
					5.						
							6.				

Across

3. Hippo is short for ____________________.
5. A hippo's body is shaped like a ____________________.
6. A hippo lives near ____________________.

Down

1. During the day, a hippo likes to ____________________.
2. The hippo looks for grass at ____________________.
4. The hippo lives in ____________________.
5. A hippo's mouth is ____________________.

Word Box			
hippopotamus	Africa	night	rest
barrel	water	big	

Name ______________________________

A Happy Hippo

Color, cut out, and paste the hippo pieces. Write something inside the hippo's mouth that would make a hippo happy.

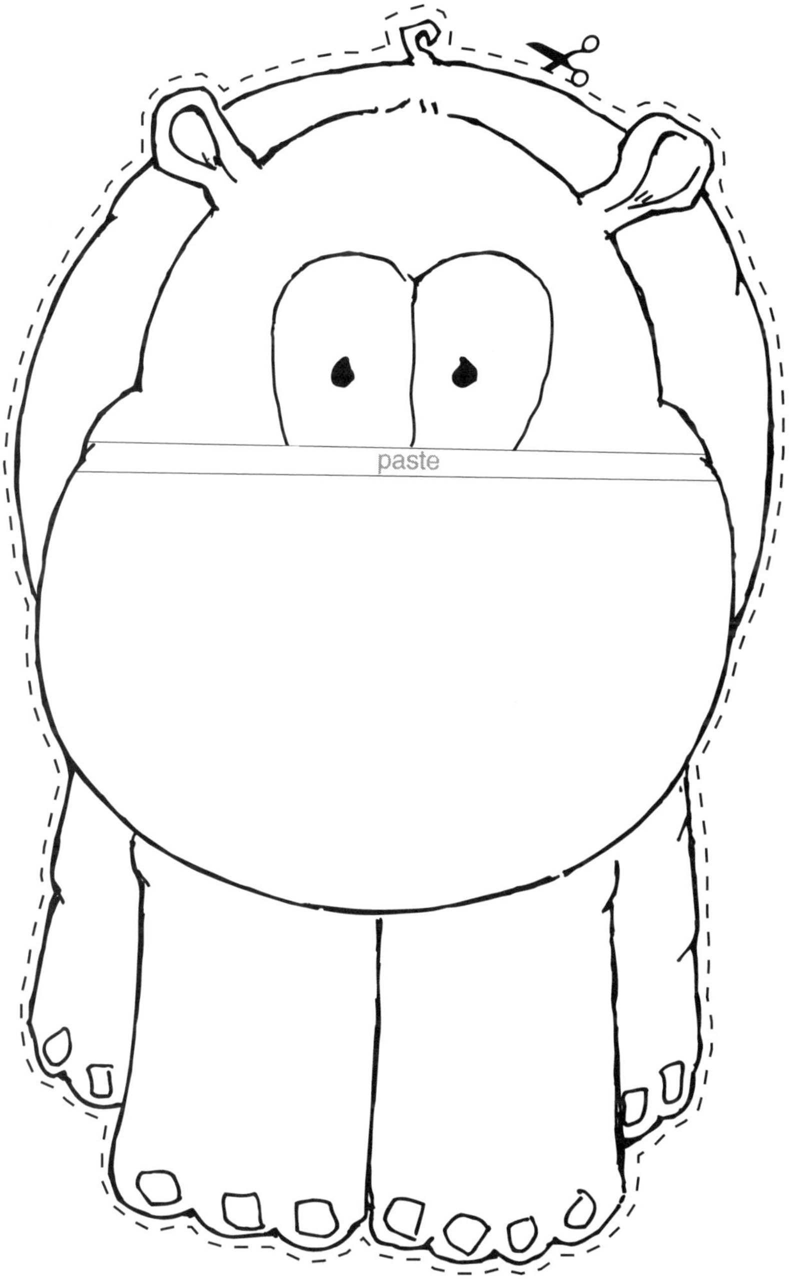

paste

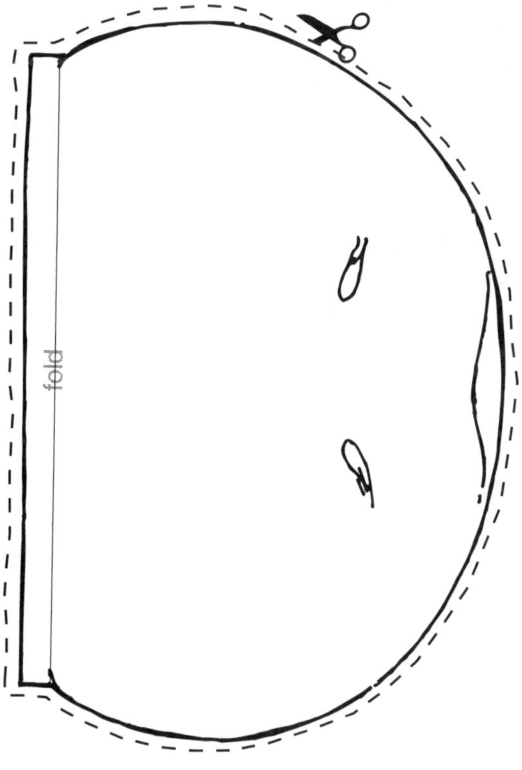

fold

Answer Key

Page 6

pictures of socks,
shoes, and mittens
(The last picture will vary.)

Page 8

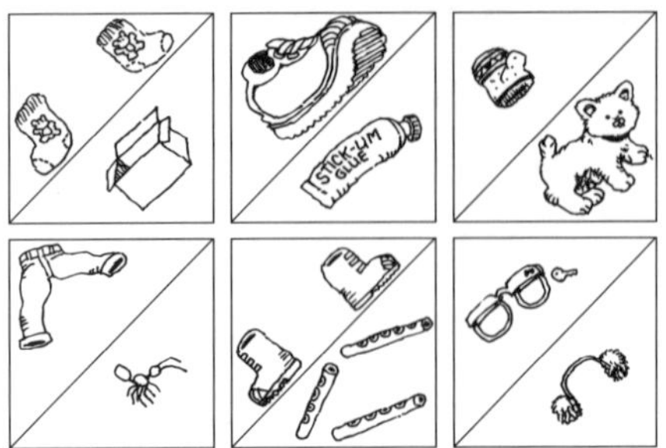

Page 9

Yes Yes
No No
No Yes

Page 12

2 1 3

Page 14

Page 15

No Yes
No Yes
Yes No

Page 18

pictures of gum ball machine,
parking meter, cup,
piggy bank, pocket, purse
(Three additional pictures
will vary.)

Page 19

A dot is a little circle.
A cot is a little bed.
The man shot an arrow.
The horse can trot.
I put the soup in the pot.
I am not going to bed now.

Page 20

Page 24

Josh's bike is red.
Josh's bike is fast.
Josh's bike wobbles.
The bike belongs to Josh.

Page 27

The seat belongs to the bike.
The hat belongs to the boy.
The wings belong to the jet.
The house belonged to his dad.
The rack belonged to the store.

Page 30

a picture of three eggs

Page 31

Page 36

chair—cat
door—pup
bed—boy
Students should draw picture of boy playing with the cat and the dog.

Page 39

napping, snoozes, hibernates, dozes

Page 42

blow bang
join

Page 43

Where will the airplane land? (Answers will vary.)
Which hand do you write with? (Answers will vary.)
Do you like to dig in the sand? (Answers will vary.)

Page 44

Page 48

Snickers loves to explore, nibble, and nap or snuggle. (Fourth answer will vary.)

Page 54

The problem was that the little person was too small to see. When he was lifted onto the shoulders he could then see.

Page 60

1. Stuff the head.
2. Put on the hat.
3. Stuff the shirt.
4. Stuff the pants.
5. Stand it up.

Page 63

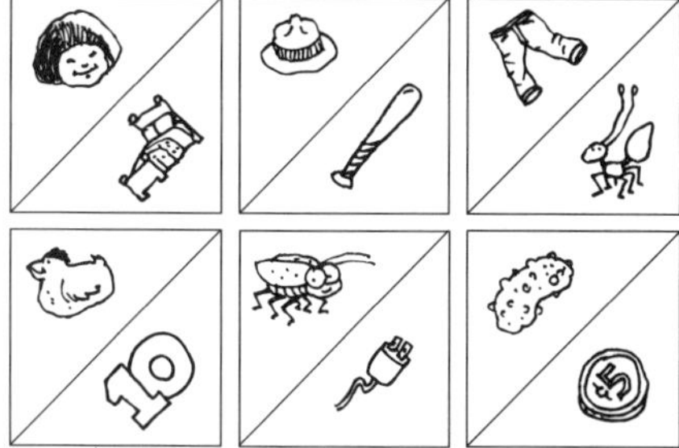

Page 66

(sheriff) saved the (gold)
(knight) saved the (princess)
(Student pictures and explanations will vary.)

Page 68

The house will be sold.
He had a cold.
The necklace is gold.
Fold the paper.

Page 69

Page 72

picture of two squirrels, picture of two dolphins, picture of twins (The fourth picture will vary.)

Page 73

squirrel, trees, sisters, dolphin, tree, squirrels, dolphins, sister

Page 74

on the rock, in the shell, on the sand, in the water

Page 78

1. They planted seeds.
2. They picked carrots.
3. They ate a snack.

The seeds were planted in the field with a tractor and in the garden by hand.
They used different containers to carry the carrots.
They all ate carrots.

Page 79

I put the photo in a frame.
Hide and Seek is my favorite game.
My grandpa came to see me.
The tame kitten licked my hand.
(Individual sentences will vary.)

Page 80

great-grandpa dad
grandpa girl
grand + son
grand + mother
grand + father
grand + daughter
grand + parent
grand + child
grand + pa
grand + ma

Page 84

First

Third

Second

Fourth

Page 90

1. Shape a ball.
2. Roll it big.
3. Make another ball.
4. Add a twig.
5. Make another ball.
6. Add two eyes and a hat.

Page 92

Page 96

City—Horns honk. Lights flash. Trains rumble. The moon shines.
Country—Chickens roost. Horses whinny. The moon shines.

Page 97

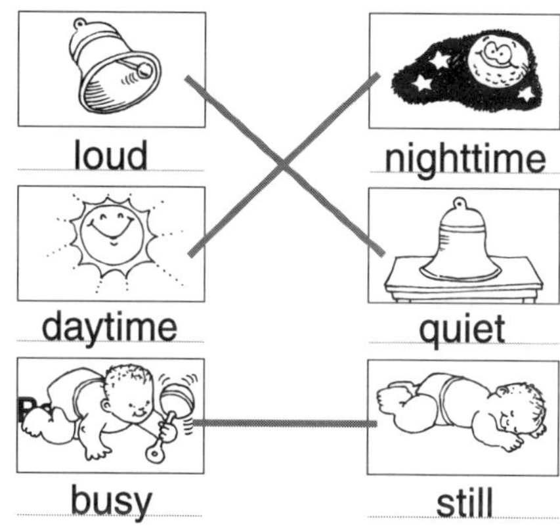

Page 98

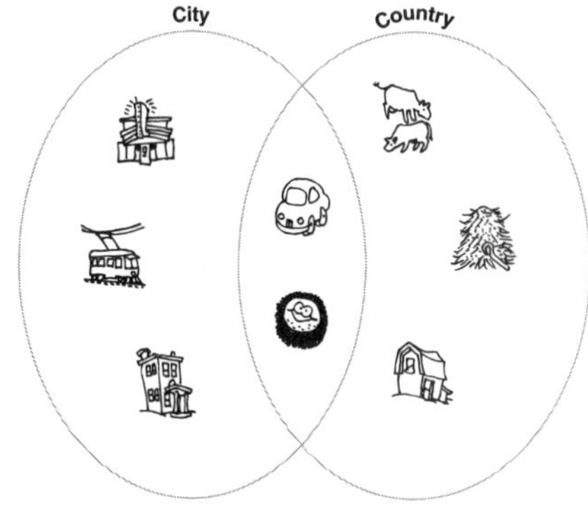

Page 102

Chelsea
Tori
Chelsea
Tori
Chelsea

Chelsea likes exciting rides and is not frightened at the amusement park. Tori prefers home to the amusement park.

Page 104

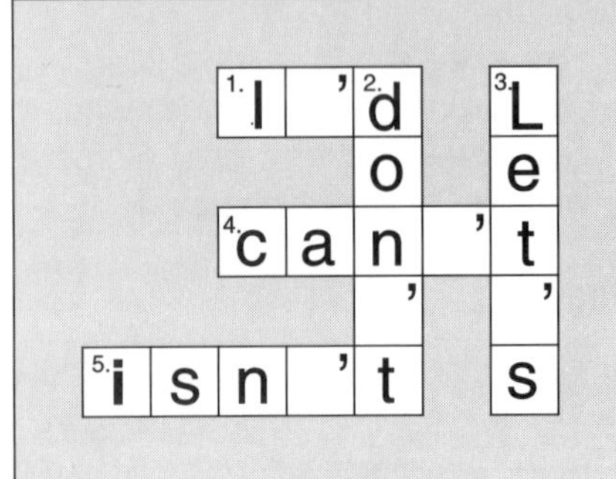

Page 108

on a bike, in a car, on a bus, on a train, in a plane
to the store, to Grandma's
(Additional answers will vary.)

Page 109

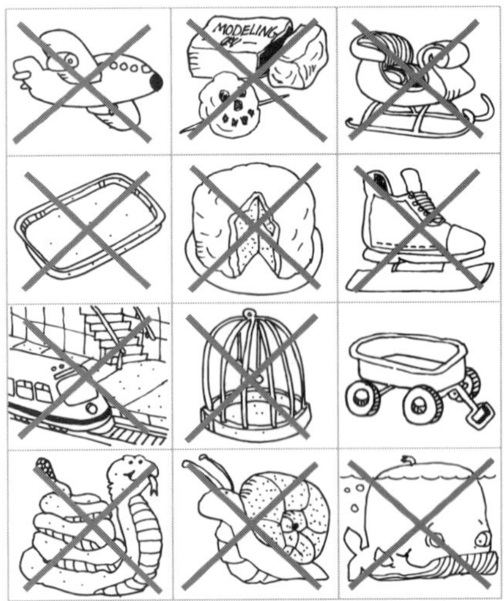

Page 110

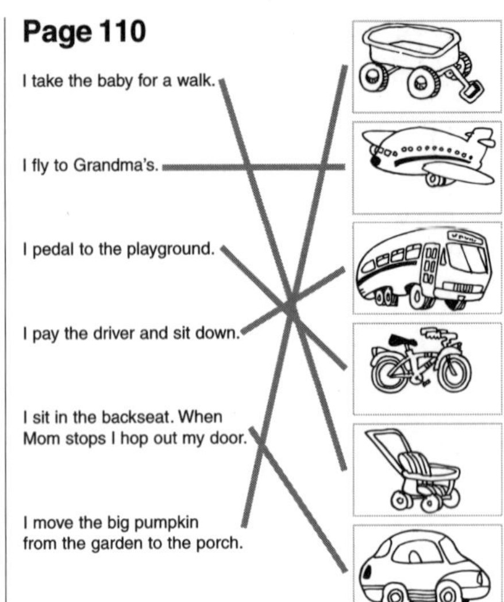

Page 114

gum balls, peppermint stick candy, cookies
yes—his or her stomach is growling
(Individual answers will vary.)

Page 115

sour	sweet
sour	sweet
sweet	sour

Page 116

Page 117

		X	X		X
			X		X
	X		X		X
			X	X	X
			X	X	

Page 120

Should show pictures of planting, flying kite, kicking a soccer ball, walking with stilts, riding a bike, foot hiking

Page 121

Page 122

Page 126

A ramp is an inclined plane.
A screw holds things together.
A lever makes lifting a lid easy.
Simple machines help us do work.
A pulley can lift something heavy.
A wheel makes moving easy.